Who the Hell is Aristotle?

Who the Hell is Aristotle?

And what are his theories all about?

Amanda Forshaw

BOWDEN
&BRAZIL

First published in Great Britain in 2020 by
Bowden & Brazil Ltd
Felixstowe, Suffolk, UK.

ISBN 978-1-8382286-2-0

Series editor & academic advisor: Dr. Jonathan C.P. Birch, University of Glasgow.

To find out more about other books and authors in this series,
visit www.whothehellis.co.uk

Contents

Introduction

Whenever you turn on a television and see an advert, or look at a billboard, or watch a political speech or a Hollywood film, you are seeing the legacy of Aristotle in action. Aristotle's *Poetics* and *Rhetoric*, written in the fourth century BCE, are still required reading for aspiring speakers and screenwriters everywhere.

Aristotle is one of the most important and influential philosophers who has ever lived. In his own time, the Ancient Greek world, he was hugely influential and as Greek philosophers go, he is only equalled by Plato, his teacher, mentor and rival. Beyond his own time Aristotle continued to have an enormous influence on ideas in both Europe and the Middle East, particularly during the Middle Ages, where he was simply known as 'the philosopher'. His influence has been, in part, due to the number of works he produced (around 200 treatises, of which approximately 30 survive) and partly due to the breadth of his investigations which covered every aspect of the human condition from logic and science to politics, ethics and aesthetics.

More than any of philosophy's founding fathers, it was Aristotle who came to be recognized as the preeminent philosopher in Medieval Christianity in the West. As interpreted by St. Thomas

Aquinas (1225–1275), Aristotle provided the resources for cosmological and design arguments for the existence of God, and for an analysis of human nature which continues to influence Roman Catholic theology.

This book can only be an introduction to his ideas and arguments such is their range and breadth. Add to that 2000 years of interpretation by many different traditions, and it makes even the basic interpretations sometimes a matter for debate. We cannot even be sure that the works that have survived were meant for publication. It is thought that what has come down to us are actually Aristotle's lecture notes or notes for works in progress or drafts; it is difficult to be sure. But from them we can get a sense of the incredible power of Aristotle's mind which places him at the forefront of the Greek Philosophers and in the triumvirate with Socrates and Plato. His works on biology, logic, rhetoric, politics and ethics are still studied and valued more than two thousand years after his death.

Who the Hell is Aristotle? looks at his life and his influences before introducing his fundamental thoughts and ideas and his most popular works, explaining them in an accessible and easy to understand way. Whether you are a student studying his works for your course, or are simply wanting to understand what all the fuss surrounding this great thinker is all about, this book will take you through the brilliant and enlightening thinking of one of the most famous philosophers in world history.

1. Aristotle's Life Story

Despite being one of the most famous philosophers of all time, Aristotle's life is not well documented. As with all men and women in ancient times, little of their personal life has come down to us. However, we do know some things about who he was and what he did during his lifetime and can therefore put together a relatively convincing picture of his upbringing, experiences and environment.

Early Life

Aristotle was born in 384 BCE into a wealthy and well-connected family in Stagira, a town on the coast of Thrace (it is 96 km from Thessaloniki, now in the popular holiday destination of Halkidiki). Stagira was a typical walled polis (an Ancient Greek city), sitting on a bluff jutting out into the Aegean Sea. The town had been part of Thrace and an ally to Athens during the Peloponnesian War (431–404 BCE), but by the time Aristotle was born the region was under the influence of Macedonia.

His father, Nicomachus, was court physician and friend to King Amyntas III and, although not much is known about Aristotle's childhood, it seems sensible to conclude that he spent time in the Macedonian palace. Because of his father's position,

Fig. 1 Roman copy in marble of a Greek bronze bust of Aristotle by Lysippos, c. 330 BCE, with modern alabaster mantle.

he would therefore have developed a connection with the Macedonian monarchy. Aristotle was born two years before the king's third son, Philip, who succeeded his father in 359 BCE as Phillip II, and it is tempting to imagine the young Aristotle and the young prince growing up together in the Macedonian court. However, it may be that by the time Aristotle was born his father had retired from his position at court and settled in Stagira. Although this is speculation, the later relationship between Aristotle and Phillip and the position of Nicomachus in the court, means it is not without foundation.

Although his father died when he was a boy, Aristotle's mother, Phaestis, and his guardian, Proxenus of Atarneus, ensured that he was able to continue his education. Not much is known about Phaestis except that she was a descendent of one of the founders of Stagira and her family owned property in Chalcis. It seems possible that she had also died by the time Aristotle was a young man. Aristotle had at least one sibling – an older sister, Arimneste, who married Proxenus (Aristotle's guardian) and with whom she had a daughter, Hero, and a son Nicanor. Hero's son, Callisthenes, would later become a student of his great-uncle Aristotle and be recommended to the service of Alexander the Great.

Whatever his family circumstances, Aristotle would have enjoyed the typical education and upbringing of a wealthy young man: language and literature from Homer and Hesiod, rhetoric, poetry and writing. As it was tradition for the son of Asclepeion physicians to follow in his father's footsteps, it is also likely that, before he died, Nicomachus would have instructed Aristotle in biological teachings as part of his son's training to one day become a doctor. The profession kept its knowledge of medicine within its circle and its secrets were passed from father to son. Had Aristotle's father lived, then it would have been almost certain that his son would have become a doctor. However, Nicomachus's death freed Aristotle from a medical career and allowed him to pursue his own interests.

In 367 BCE, when Aristotle was just 17, Proxenus took him to complete his education at Plato's Academy in Athens. This move was to have profound consequences for Aristotle and, indeed, the whole of Western philosophy.

The Academy and Athens

Aristotle's reason for leaving home for Athens was probably not just academic. Amyntas III died in 370 BCE and, after 20 years of peace, the monarchy descended into the internecine rivalry which had characterized much of Aristotle's history; suddenly a connection to the late king was not an advantage and so Aristotle's departure for Athens was a good political move.

When Aristotle arrived in Athens, he was entering the largest city in Greece. By the beginning of the fifth century BCE, Athens had a population of around 100,000 inhabitants, double the size of its nearest rivals. Despite coming from a good

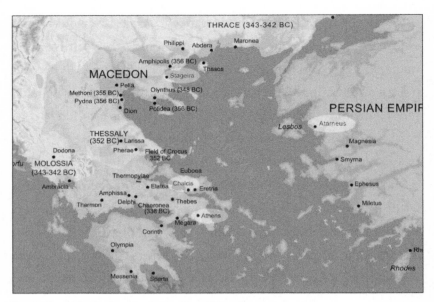

Fig. 2 Map of the Ancient Greek Kingdom of Macedon.

background, Aristotle would have been seen as a Macedonian and a country bumpkin by most Athenians. In 450 BCE a law was passed which stated that to be a citizen of Athens both parents must be Athenian. As a foreigner living in the city, Aristotle was classed as a 'metic' which meant that he had to pay a special tax and have a citizen sponsor (it is not known who his citizen sponsor was, but it is thought to have been Plato). While a metic had some legal protection, he could not vote in the Assembly, nor could he own property. This is not to say that metics could not become wealthy and influential, but they would never be fully accepted as Athenian. Despite spending a large part of his life teaching and living in Athens, Aristotle was always an outsider and, as Macedonia's influence grew, there was the danger that his connection to her monarchy would make him a figure of suspicion.

But in 367 BCE Aristotle was a young student, attracted by all the opportunities that Athens had to offer, and a chance to study at Plato's Academy. The Academy, founded in 387 BCE, was one of the most important centres for learning in the ancient world. When Aristotle arrived, Plato (who was then in his late fifties; Plato was born either in 428 BCE or 424 BCE) made a journey to Syracuse to work with his old friend Dion in shaping the education of the young King Dionysus II. However, neither Dion nor Plato's influence seemed to have had a positive effect on the young king. Plato and Dion became embroiled in political intrigues which resulted in Dion's exile and Plato's house arrest. So, for the first two years of Aristotle's stay at the Academy he was under the instruction of Eudoxus of Cnidus.

Plato returned to Athens in around 365 BCE, at which point we can safely assume he met with Aristotle for the first time. Their relationship was to last for the next 20 years and was to become one of the most iconic in philosophy. Once he had finished studying, Aristotle became a teacher at the Academy, where he would remain for the next 20 years.

Leaving Athens

In 347 BCE Aristotle left Athens. The reasons for leaving are not clear but Plato's death in 348 BCE led to his nephew, Speusippus, taking control of the Academy and it may be that Aristotle and Speusippus had different ideas about the direction that the Academy should take after Plato. But perhaps a more compelling reason was Aristotle's Macedonian connection. In 348 BCE, the town of Olynthus had fallen to the Macedonian army, led by Philip II. As a result, Demosthenes had come to power in Athens on a wave of anti-Macedonian feeling and Aristotle may well have felt it wise to leave the city rather than face any backlash.

Aristotle and his companions sailed east to Atarneus which was ruled by Hermias, a friend of Macedonia and a great supporter of philosophy. Hermias allowed Aristotle and his friends to settle in the city of Assos where they spent the next few years discussing philosophy and undertaking research into the natural sciences. It was at this time that Aristotle met and married Pythias, Hermias' niece. The couple had a child, who they called Pythias the younger, but sadly the marriage was not to last long as Pythias died young, possibly around 335 BCE. Aristotle was later to find another companion, Herpyllis, from his hometown Stagira, although it is not thought that they married. They did however have a son, Nicomachus, who they named after Aristotle's father.

At some point during this time Aristotle travelled to Lesbos, accompanied by Theophrastus, where they continued their scientific research by analyzing the zoology and botany of the island. Aristotle's stay in Assos came to an end when the Persians attacked the town and executed Hermias. Aristotle and his family managed to escape, and it is thought that they returned home to Stagira sometime before 343 BCE, when Philip II of Macedon invited Aristotle to become tutor to his son, Alexander.

Aristotle and Alexander the Great

Alexander was 13 when Aristotle arrived at Pella, the Macedonian capital, to become his tutor. Philip had several reasons for choosing Aristotle. Not only was Aristotle a product of the Academy and a well-known tutor and researcher in his own right, but he had, in his youth, been connected to the Macedonian court, and was

Fig. 3 Alexander and Aristotle, illustration by Charles Laplante, 1866

possibly a childhood friend of Philip's. He had also recently been living in Atarneus as a guest of Hermias, one of Philip's allies.

In the years of Aristotle's absence from Macedonia, Philip had succeeded in extending Macedonian influence over Thrace in the east and Greece in the south, as well as re-organizing local government, strengthening the army and increasing the royal treasury with the acquisition of the lucrative gold mines at Krinides, which he subsequently called Philippi after himself. He also built the first Macedonian navy. Alexander was born in Pella in 356 BCE but Philip felt that the capital was not a good environment for study and so he sent the young prince, his tutor and his companions to the Precinct of the Nymphs at Mieza where they could study in rural solitude away from the distractions of the court.

Aristotle undoubtedly passed many of his ideas on to Alexander; however, it is not clear how studying with Aristotle influenced the

Fig. 4 Aristotle founded his Peripatetic school in 335 BCE between the rivers Iridanos and Ilissos, outside the city walls of Athens.

young mind of the prince. There are no surviving books, letters, papers or any other works which document the teachings that took place in Mieza. However, the Greek author, Plutarch, noted that 'for a while [Alexander] loved and cherished Aristotle no less [...] than if he had been his father, giving this reason for it: that as he had received life from the one, so the other had taught him to live well' (Plutarch, *Life of Alexander*, c. 100 AD). Aristotle continued his role as tutor until Alexander ascended to the throne in 336 BCE. By 335 BCE, Aristotle had returned to Athens, although the two men remained in contact through letters.

Return to Athens and the Lyceum

The death of Philip II freed the young Alexander to follow his ambition to increase Macedonian power and influence. It also allowed Aristotle to leave Pella and return to Athens to fulfil his own dream of opening his own place of learning, one to rival the Academy. Aristotle was about 50 when he returned to Athens with his family and his best student, Theophrastus. Like the Academy, the Lyceum was on the outskirts of Athens – north-east of the city – and was named after Apollo Lyceus, the wolf-god. The school, which was dedicated to the Muses (the inspirational goddesses of literature, science and the arts), was also called the Peripatetic (from *peripatoi*, a walk, or *peripateo*, walking), probably because of Aristotle's habit of walking or strolling while teaching his students. Aristotle's Lyceum was not a college or university as we would know it today, it was – as Jonathan Barnes describes in *Aristotle* (1986) – 'a sort of public leisure centre'. It served as a library, lecture hall, gym, military training ground and research centre; there were no exams or degrees and, it seems, no fees or even official students. The Lyceum was a centre of learning in all its forms, providing a place of knowledge for both academics and the general public, to whom Aristotle would deliver public lectures in the evenings. For the next 13 years Aristotle was to produce an astonishing variety and volume of work, some of which will be discussed in later chapters.

Flight from Athens and Death

During Aristotle's years at the Lyceum, his relationship with his former pupil Alexander apparently cooled. Alexander became more and more megalomaniacal, finally proclaiming himself divine and demanding that Greeks prostrate themselves before him in adoration. Opposition to this demand was led by Aristotle's great-nephew, Callisthenes (360–327 BCE), who had been appointed historian of Alexander's Asiatic expedition on Aristotle's recommendation. For his heroism Callisthenes was falsely implicated in a plot and executed.

When Alexander died in 323 BCE, there was an anti-Macedonian backlash in Athens and Aristotle left the city for a second time, apparently saying that he did not wish the city that had executed Socrates to sin twice against philosophy. Aristotle went to Chalcis where his mother's family owned land and he died there a year later in 332 BCE.

Aristotle's will has survived. In it he made provisions for several friends and dependents, including his son Nicomachus and his daughter Pythias. Theophrastus succeeded him as the head of the Lyceum and Aristotle left him his library including his vast collection of writings. Unfortunately, his surviving works amount to only around one million words – a fraction of his output in life.

Aristotle's Timeline

Aristotle (BCE)	World Events (BCE)
	428 Plato is born in Athens
	399 Trial and death of Socrates
	392 Amyntas III becomes king of Macedonia
	388 Plato opens the Academy
384 Aristotle is born in Stagira, northern Greece	
c.374 Nicomachus, Aristotle's father, dies	
371 Proxenus of Atarneus becomes Aristotle's guardian	
	370 Amyntas III of Macedonia dies
367 Aristotle moves to Athens to attend Plato's Academy	
	359 Philip II becomes king of Macedonia
	356 Alexander the Great is born
	348 Stagira is conquered by Philip II
347 Aristotle leaves Athens and travels to the court of Hermias of Atarneus	347 Plato dies and Speusippus becomes head of the Academy
c.346 Aristotle marries Pythias	
	345 Hermias is killed by Persians
344 Aristotle travels to Lesbos and starts researching the great lagoon	
343 Aristotle starts tutoring Alexander of Macedonia in Pella	

340 Aristotle stops tutoring Alexander	
	339 Speusippus dies
	338 Philip II defeats the Greeks and the Hellenic League is formed
	336 Philip II is assassinated
335 Aristotle travels to Athens and opens the Lyceum	**335** Alexander defeats the Thracians
335-323 Aristotle is believed to have written his major works during this period	**334** Alexander campaigns in Asia Minor
335-326 Pythias dies and Aristotle lives with Herpyllis	**332** Alexander conquers Egypt
	331 Alexander attacks Persia
	327/6 Alexander invades Afghanistan and Pakistan
325 Aristotle's son Nicomachus is born	
323/2 Aristotle travels to Chalcis	**323** Alexander the Great dies
322 Aristotle dies	

2. Influences on Aristotle's Thinking

Aristotle lived at a vibrant time for philosophy and the development of ideas, not least because he formed the greatest triumvirate of thinkers together with Socrates and Plato. Aristotle's study at the Academy involved ideas from both these men but also built on earlier traditions. Aristotle himself may have discarded some ideas and indeed disagreed with his mentor, but the canon of Greek thought formed his education and the basis of his thinking – in knowing the theories and ideas of the time he could debunk them.

The Pre-Socratics

Although we talk about the pre-Socratics as a group, these philosophers who came before Socrates in the sixth and fifth centuries BCE were not homogenous. They came from different traditions and places and differed on key theories and ideas. However, as a group they introduced new ways of thinking and have been identified as the first philosophers and scientists of the Western tradition. The term 'pre-Socratic' was coined in the eighteenth century and came into common use in the nineteenth century but it is quite a controversial one. The term is supposed to divide those philosophers who focused on cosmological and physical ideas from Socrates and those that followed him who focused more on ethics and moral problems. However, this division does not stand up to scrutiny as the pre-Socratics often also considered ethical arguments and some were contemporaries of Socrates, Plato and Aristotle. Perhaps the best way to think of them is as the group of ancient philosophers who were not influenced by the ideas of Socrates.

Each of the pre-Socratics wrote at least one key work but very few have survived and none in their entirety. Much of what we know of them and their ideas has come down to us through the work of later writers such as Plato, Aristotle and Theophrastus. Aristotle often referenced the pre-Socratics in the context of his own philosophy, surveying their ideas before setting out to write his own thoughts on a particular topic. While he sometimes agreed with their thinking, he more often than not disagreed. Because no complete writings exist from any of the pre-Socratics, we are not able to read their actual ideas first-hand in their entirety. Therefore, it is impossible to know whether Aristotle's arguments represented the pre-Socratics fairly and accurately and whether he properly addressed or refuted their theories.

Piecing together some of their key ideas, we know that the pre-Socratics thought of themselves as inquirers into a vast range of topics and subjects. They had views on the nature of the world, the nature of the cosmos, the natural world, physics, chemistry and biology as well as ethics, metaphysics and theology. They were asking the big questions about the nature of reality, the structure of the universe, and astronomy, and they were diverse and independent thinkers. No aspect of human existence was ignored by these early searchers for knowledge and it is their inquiries that became the basis of what Plato and Aristotle were later to call philosophy.

There are in the region of 20 philosophers and schools of thought that might be included in this group but here we will focus only on a few key people and influential ideas.

The Milesians

The Milesian thinkers, Thales (c. 624–525 BCE), Anaximander (c. 610–545 BCE) and Anaximenes (c. 586–528 BCE) all came from Miletus in Ionia (now in Turkey). This geographical position makes it possible that they travelled to Egypt or Babylon – both civilizations that had an impact on early Greek philosophy. Apart from a birthplace, the three philosophers shared an interest in investigating celestial and terrestrial phenomena and explaining them in naturalistic terms rather than in terms of legend or mythology. What we know about Thales is restricted to anecdotes and stories, but we do know that he focused much of his work on geometry, the cosmos and the beginning of things. According to Aristotle in his *Metaphysics*, Thales was the first to look at causes and principles of natural phenomena and the natural world, proclaiming water to be the first cause. Anaximander also investigated the origins of the cosmos but argued that it was the elements in the universe (for him this was an infinite underlying, boundless reality), which are continually coming together and breaking apart. Anaximenes agreed with Anaximander that some boundless power underlies everything, but he believed that this energy was known and that it was air. While the Milesians did not abandon their belief in the gods, they brought about a change in thinking that was distinctly more scientific.

Another Milesian thinker, Xenophanes (c. 570–478 BCE), who came from north of Miletus, explicitly challenged traditional explanations of the universe and the beginning of things. He rejected dogma and promoted the idea of rational and critical thought which was to continue and develop long after him.

Pythagoras

While the Milesians are credited for offering explanations on the basis of matter, Aristotle saw Pythagoras as doing the same with number. Pythagoras (c. 570–490 BCE) is a familiar name to any student of geometry, and while very little is known about Pythagoras the man, what we do know is that a following developed in his name which was to continue long after his death and to have a clear impact on Platonic thought. Pythagoras grew up not far from Miletus so it is more than possible that he would have known about the Milesian philosophers and even studied at their academy. Pythagoras was deeply religious; he believed in reincarnation and established a religious cult in Croton in southern Italy where he and his followers adhered to strict behavioural and dietary rules. They believed the only way to stop the endless cycle of reincarnation, which was the main goal of life, was to live a life in contemplation of scientific thinking. Pythagoras saw God-given truths in geometry and mathematics and saw mathematical proofs as evidence of divine revelation.

His mathematical discoveries were the product of pure reasoning and it is his idea that the cosmos is governed by mathematical rules that was to become so influential for later philosophers such as Plato. Pythagoras explained the creation of the universe in mathematical form; that God created a measurable unity from which everything else was formed. His argument can be summed up thus: Everything in the universe conforms to mathematical rules; if we can understand mathematical relationships then we can understand the structure of the cosmos. Therefore, mathematics is the key to philosophical thought.

Heraclitus and Parmenides

While these two philosophers were contemporaries, they disagreed on the nature of the cosmos. Heraclitus (c. 535–475 BCE) argued that everything in the universe was in a constant state of flux. Day turns into night which turns back into day again. He gave a well-known example of 'you can never step into the same river twice'; the river is described as a fixed unchanging thing (like the cosmos) and yet the moment you step into it, the water that you have placed your foot into will be replaced by fresh water. What then, is 'the river'? This idea of flux influenced Plato, although he and Aristotle both dismissed Heraclitus' arguments as being contradictory.

Parmenides (c. 515–445 BCE) is a key figure in pre-Socratic thought and is considered to be one of the most influential thinkers on the whole history of Western philosophy. According to Richard McKirahan (2010) Parmenides is the inventor of metaphysics, the enquiry into the nature of being and reality. Parmenides moved beyond the evidence of his senses and used deductive reasoning to uncover the physical nature of the universe. For example, he theorized that something that exists cannot also not exist and therefore the state of nothing existing is impossible. As something (in this case the cosmos) cannot come from nothing, it must have always existed. One of the key ideas that Parmenides demonstrates that had a significant influence on later philosophers is that we can never completely rely on the experience given to us by our senses. Our perception of the world is faulty and full of contradictions.

Zeno and Anaxagoras

Zeno (c. 490–430 BCE), who Aristotle considered to be the inventor of the dialectic (a debate which excludes emotion and focuses on logic), is worth mentioning for his paradoxes. A student, and possibly boyfriend, of Parmenides, Zeno focused on investigating the relationship between logical argument and the evidence of the senses. He developed four famous paradoxes of motion which claim to show that, despite the evidence around us, the ordinary motion of everyday experiences are impossible; that motions can never be begun (Achilles and the Tortoise) or completed (The Dichotomy) and they either entail contradictions (The Moving Rows) or are impossible (The Arrow).

Anaxagoras of Clazomenae (c. 500–428 BCE) died around the time that Plato was born but his ideas continued to spark interest in his philosophical successors. Some accused him of being an atheist because he argued that heavenly bodies such as the sun and moon were fiery stones and not divine beings. Plato and Aristotle, however, were excited by his idea of a unifying cosmic principle that wasn't based upon divine intervention and hoped to discover, through his writings, the answer to how and why the cosmos came into being. However, they were to be disappointed as Anaxagoras never went beyond mechanistic explanatory details. He developed explanations of the world that were purely naturalistic, using his senses to investigate the nature of things, and his mind to look beyond the senses for the cause. Aristotle, while praising him as an original thinker, complained in his *Metaphysics*: 'When he cannot explain why something is necessarily as it is, he drags in Mind, but otherwise he will use anything rather than Mind to explain a particular phenomenon.'

Other ideas of Anaxagoras included the suggestion that all generated objects, such as human beings, plants and planets, were temporary mixtures of ingredients such as earth, air, fire, flesh, water etc. that are existing but in constant motion. He attributed the motion of these things to an intelligent force.

The Atomists

The atomists, Leucippus (early fifth century BCE) and Democritus (c. 460–370 BCE) began a legacy in scientific thought that developed into modern philosophy. These philosophers argued that everything is made up of tiny indivisible particles (atoms from the Greek *atomos*, meaning 'uncuttable'). A void separates the atoms and allows them to move freely colliding with each other, forming patterns and arrangements and then breaking away again. This is why, they suggested, objects in the world appear to change. The reason there seems to be some fixed substances is because, while there are an infinite number of atoms, there is a fixed number of ways in which they can arrange themselves.

This theory, known as atomism, we can clearly recognize as being influential in our own time and, in the fifth century BCE, it gave the first mechanistic view of the universe. It also identified fundamental properties of matter. This idea that all atoms are made of the same solid matter was taken up by Aristotle in the *Metaphysics* where he argued that atoms only differ from each other in shape, position and arrangement. The Atomists argued that atoms are responsible for sense perception and thought; particular shaped atoms cause taste, sight, touch, hearing and smell. They believed that we do not perceive things in themselves, what we perceive are atoms and the void; how we interpret them is a matter of opinion and convention.

The pre-Socratic philosophers were a varied group whose interests ranged from religion to the nature of things, ethics to mathematics. We have only touched on a small portion of their thought here, but we can see that they passed on questions and answers that became the basic concerns of Plato and Aristotle and, after them, the concern of Western philosophy as a whole. We now come to the two most important influences on Aristotle and on the philosophical tradition in which he lived and worked and as such we will spend some time looking at their ideas.

Socrates

Socrates (469–399 BCE) is considered to be one of the founders of Western philosophy and yet he wrote no treatise; he did not start a school and does not seem to have held any particular theories of his own. Why then was he so important? What Socrates did was to ask questions. He asked questions that interested him, and he pursued those questions in an effort to examine the basis of the concepts that we apply to ourselves. Socrates believed that understanding what we are is the first step in philosophy. He developed a new way of thinking which bears his name: the Socratic method, or the dialectic, which is a way of examining beliefs and concepts through question and answer.

We have both Xenophon (c. 430–354 BCE) – a student of Socrates – and Plato to thank for recording Socrates' ideas, although many scholars believe that Plato's 'dialogues', (the *Apology*, the *Phaedo*, the *Symposium*, to name a few) are the most accurate in their depiction of the historical Socrates. In Plato's dialogues, Socrates investigated ideas such as the nature of justice, what it is to live a good life, and how to question our fundamental beliefs about ourselves and others. 'The unexamined life is not worth living' is one of his most famous sayings. What he meant by this was that the only life worth living is a good life. A good life is only possible by knowing what 'good' and 'evil' actually are. Socrates argued that good and evil were not relative (as some of the pre-Socratics had argued) but were absolutes that could be discovered through questioning and reason. If we do not question, then we live in ignorance without morality but if we live a life of examination then we will discover both morality and knowledge.

It is impossible to overestimate the influence Socrates had on Plato and Aristotle; he was the towering philosophical figure of his time. While a student at the Academy, Aristotle would have studied Socrates' method through the teachings of Plato. In the following chapters we will see how Aristotle began with Socrates' ideas before taking them in his own direction.

In Plato's *Phaedrus*, the discussion revolves around the art of rhetoric and how it should be practised. For Socrates, philosophy was not about rhetoric, but about the dialectic; it was the art of having a conversation. His method was quizzing, the science of working towards truth through question and answer. Socrates would wander around, stop people and ask them a question about virtue or justice or a moral value and then he would lead them into a discussion which usually undermined the person's assumptions. He prioritized definitions – prodding people to define and redefine.

Aristotle considered the importance of definitions to be one of Socrates' most important contributions to the development of philosophical method. Socrates considered the question, 'what is it?' to be the most important thing you can ask about anything. After all, if you don't know what it is, then you can't answer any more questions nor develop your argument any further. For example, if we ask the question: Does justice benefit the person that possesses it? We can't answer this question until we know what justice is.

Socrates' passion was for ethics. He believed that in order to discover our true nature we must look inward in search of self-knowledge. Contrary to his contemporaries, Socrates believed our true self to be our soul. He therefore believed that human beings should prioritize taking care of the soul which he considered to be more important than the body or external goods (by which he meant appearance, reputation, wealth etc.). He believed that nothing external can do you any good unless you exercise it virtuously. Socrates considered the soul to be immortal, to be that which animates the body, and after death, to animate another body. In Chapter 5 we will look at Aristotle's own definition of the soul.

Perhaps one of most influential aspects of Socrates' thought, not only on Aristotle but also on later classical schools of thought such as the Stoics, was the idea of how to live the good life. He believed that to live a flourishing life is to live the virtuous life. The argument that knowledge allows you to understand what it is to achieve the good life, as we will see, becomes a key notion in the development of Aristotle's ethics (see Chapter 4).

Flourishing (or in Greek, *eudaimonia*) is difficult to translate, but essentially it means actualizing your potential and being a successful human being. For example, if you hurt others, you are hurting yourself; if you do not live virtuously then you are damaging your own soul. But what did Socrates mean by virtue exactly? For Socrates, virtue is a sort of knowledge, similar to the skill needed for a particular craft. He believed that there are five virtues – wisdom, temperance, courage, justice and piety – and that they form a unity as, while each is a different kind of knowledge, all are inseparable. What this means is that if a human possesses one of the virtues, then they automatically possess them all; they possess expert knowledge of what is good and what is bad. So, if virtue is knowledge then vice is ignorance – no-one does wrong willingly, they do wrong because they are ignorant. If you have knowledge, then you know what to do. The way Socrates lived his own life seemed to exemplify this idea: by living a simple life, spending his time thinking and teaching and pursuing knowledge, Socrates was able to make rational decisions without being swayed by his emotions. It is this focus on knowledge and virtue as opposed to pursuing wealth and position that demonstrates Socrates' 'good life', and it is this that Aristotle thinks of when exploring his ideas of virtue.

Plato

Plato (c. 427–347 BCE) was Aristotle's teacher and, later on, his colleague. He clearly had an enormous effect on his pupil as, even though Aristotle was to reject many of Plato's ideas, his influence is seen throughout Aristotle's thinking, particularly in metaphysics and ethics. Plato was an Athenian nobleman who gave himself up to the study and teaching of philosophy. His works can be roughly divided into three periods. His early period featured much of what is known about Socrates: most of these works are written in the form of dialogues, using the Socratic method as the basis for teaching. Plato's second or middle period is comprised of works where he explores morality and virtue in individuals and society. He presents lengthy discussions on justice, wisdom and courage, as well as the duality of power and responsibility. Plato's most famous work, the *Republic*, which was his vision of a utopian society, was written during this period. The third period of Plato's writings mainly discusses the role of the arts, along with morality and ethics. Plato challenges his earlier conclusions through self-examination.

Theory of Forms

In his Theory of Forms Plato states that only ideas are constant, that the world perceived by senses is deceptive and changeable. As Plato's student, Aristotle would undoubtedly have discussed the Theory of Forms at length with his tutor. Ultimately, however, he disagreed with him. One of the key questions Plato asks is this: Where do my concepts of justice, morality and even of numbers come from? They are not *a posteriori* ideas (discovered from experiencing the world), as they are not derived from any sense-experience; we can't 'see', 'taste' or 'touch' justice or morality or 'infinity', we seem to just understand what these concepts mean. How do we acquire such ideas then? Plato argues, by way of his controversial Theory of Forms, that such ideas are not acquired at all: we have them in our mind from birth and use reason to remember them. For example – if we draw a circle on a piece of paper, we will not be able to draw a perfect circle. There will be some slight imperfections, even though the circle we are imagining is perfect. Plato argues that we recognize that approximate circles are circles because we have an innate idea of what a circle looks like. Similarly, we know what a just or moral act is because we have an innate understanding of what justice or morality is. We cannot define justice or morality, but our understanding proves that these are concepts that are in our minds from birth.

Aristotle fundamentally disagreed with Plato and his argument that we are born with innate knowledge. We will look at this further in Chapter 4.

In the *Republic*, Plato uses one of the most famous analogies in philosophy – the Allegory of the Cave – to explain his concept of the Forms. Essentially, Plato sets out to show a philosopher's journey from ignorance to knowledge. He sees ordinary experience as being like that of prisoners, chained to the back wall of a cave, unable to see outside. Behind them is a fire which illuminates moving objects from outside the cave and casts their shadow upon the wall. Since it is all the prisoners know, they assume that the shadows are the true forms of the objects.

Plato describes the philosopher as being like a prisoner who, escaping his chains, turns and sees first the fire and then objects being carried. He then moves up to the mouth of the cave and is dazzled by the light of the sun – which Plato calls the Form

Fig. 5 An illustration of The Allegory of the Cave from Plato's *Republic*.

of the Good and which represents the higher truth of ideas. At first blinded, the prisoner cannot make sense of what he is seeing but, forced to continue his journey out into the sunlight, his eyes adjust and he eventually sees the reality of the world.

On returning, he tries to explain to the other prisoners that their everyday experience is that of shadows, which are not real. But having become habituated to the sunlight, the prisoner is once again blinded, this time by the darkness. His fellow prisoners believe his eyes to have been affected by leaving the cave and refuse to journey out. Here Plato contrasts the prisoner (philosopher), who understands that the physical world is but a shadow of the truth, with the other prisoners (all non-philosophers) who remain ignorant in their superficial physical reality, accepting only what they see at face value.

Plato believed that most people could not be taught about the nature of the Forms since they cannot be revealed through education, they can only be recalled (remember that Plato believed such concepts to exist in our minds from birth). While Aristotle agreed that philosophers might have particular knowledge, he believed that this knowledge came from study and observation and not from recalling knowledge that is already in our minds. He did not believe that our world was only a 'shadow' of a more real world. In response to Plato's Theory of Forms, Aristotle developed his own theory – which became known as the theory of Hylomorphism – which set forth that all material substances are matter and form (see Chapter 3).

Plato's Ethics

The link between Plato and Aristotle is most obvious when it comes to their views on ethics. Plato's belief that virtue is knowledge echoed Socrates' thinking. To know the good is to do the good: in other words, knowing the right thing to do will lead to one automatically doing the right thing. This is illustrated in Plato's cave analogy, whereby the prisoner leaves the cave and 'sees' the Form of the Good. He then knows the right thing to do. Plato argues that virtue is enough for happiness.

However, as we shall see in Chapter 4, while Aristotle agreed that wisdom was virtuous, he also argued that we must *choose* to do good. So while both Plato and Aristotle considered happiness as a worthy goal, Aristotle was more practical and his theories more active, while Plato was more contemplative. Aristotle believed that wisdom is only achieved with effort. Not only is virtue needed for happiness but also for a stable society which could help create satisfaction and contentment. We can see Plato's influence in the idea of developing knowledge of what is good and the key place that wisdom holds in the understanding of morality, but Plato seems to be arguing that only a few (philosophers) will reach an understanding of morality while Aristotle argues that everyone can achieve moral knowledge.

Plato's Politics

In the *Republic*, Plato outlines a utopian society which has a structured political body with each group performing its specific function and not interfering in any other business. Plato saw this as a way to achieve a perfect form of government. In his world, the three classes – philosopher, warrior and worker – take on a particular role to enable society to function. Philosophers are the rulers, being best qualified because they have wisdom; warriors are the defenders of society and must uphold the ruler's convictions; and workers (who make up the majority of the people) are the farmers, traders, merchants, etc. who carry out, and must limit themselves to, whatever skill they possess. While Aristotle agrees with some elements of Plato's political ideas, he sees the basic political unit as the city (polis). This takes precedence over the family and the individual. The role of the polis is to create an environment where the citizens can live a good life. In politics, as in many other spheres, Aristotle differs from Plato and Socrates because he moves away from theory – theory about knowledge, ethics, the nature of the universe and politics – and investigates the practical implementation of the processes and structures suggested by the ideas.

Aristotle's New Direction

There is no doubt that Aristotle's thinking and investigations rest on the diversity of previous philosophical theories about reality and the universe. In his works we can clearly see the influence of Socrates in the structure of the argument and ideas about rhetoric and the dialectic, but it is Plato that stands out as Aristotle's main influence, not because Aristotle continued the work of his master but rather because, in some key respects, he disagreed with it.

3. The Fundamental Nature of Things

The works of Aristotle's that survived represent only a small percentage of what he wrote. He was a true polymath and the breadth of his investigations cut across all aspects of nature, the universe and the human condition. It is very difficult therefore to give more than just a suggestion of some of his thoughts. However, there are certain ideas that underpin everything that he wrote, and we will try to do justice to these over the following four chapters.

Aristotle was a prolific writer and thinker. The overriding driver throughout his life was the pursuit of knowledge. He believed that 'all men by their nature desire to know'. In the *Protrepticus* he argued that 'the acquisition of wisdom is pleasant; all men feel at home in philosophy and wish to spend time on it, leaving aside other things.'

Science Vs. Abstract Concepts

Aristotle referred to all the branches of learning as 'sciences' and it is on this basis that we can organize his work. First, *theoretical sciences*, which includes physics and mathematics but also metaphysics – the study of the nature of the universe and an explanation for the cause of all things. In Aristotelian terminology, physics includes natural sciences such as biology, zoology and astronomy. The second branch – *practical sciences* – deals with human and societal conduct. While theoretical science seeks knowledge for its own sake, practical science is about the application of that knowledge on the world as it is. The last category – *productive sciences* – focuses on human production, not just artefacts or crafts but *all* human production, including poetry, agriculture, dance, theatre, music, rhetoric, pottery, and so on.

Like his mentor, Plato, Aristotle wanted to find an anchor in a world of change; some absolute truth on which everything could be built. For Plato, this was the Theory of Forms, the two-world view that suggests that everything in this world is a mere copy of the true, ideal form that exists in another world: the realm of Forms (see Chapter 2). This other world can only be reached through the mind – can only be known conceptually – and so is only accessible by those who have knowledge, namely philosophers.

Aristotle fundamentally disagreed with this view. While Plato's background was in mathematics and he sought explanations for the world in abstract concepts, Aristotle's interest in the world was scientific. He used his observations of the world to develop ideas rooted in experience and information gained through our senses. For example, we do not recognize that a Shetland pony is a type of horse because we have knowledge of the Form of Horse. We recognize that a Shetland pony is a type of horse because we have seen horses before and, in coming across other horses, we have seen the characteristics that they have in common which enables us to recognize the same type of animal. We learn from our experiences in the world and use our reason to understand the shared characteristics of things.

Aristotle argued that what was true of things in the natural world is also true of abstract concepts and ideas. We observe human actions and see that some are just, and some are unjust. From our observations and reason, we begin to understand the characteristics that make up justice. Once we have built up a picture of these characteristics, we can observe justice, or the lack of it, in all things.

A Theory of Knowledge

Aristotle's view became the basis for one of the key divisions in the branch of philosophy called 'epistemology' – the theory of knowledge. Epistemology is concerned with what we can know, whether our knowledge can be certain and how we gain our knowledge of the world and abstract ideas.

Aristotle believed that our mind is born blank and any knowledge and concepts we gain are developed in our minds through our senses and our experience as we encounter life. He does not argue that universal qualities such as beauty or courage exist somewhere else in a perfect form, but that the way we come to know them, and their nature, is through investigation using our senses. This approach would later become known as Empiricism, and it forms the basis of modern science. Empiricism focuses on the role of empirical evidence (information from the senses and observation) in the formulation of ideas about the world. It is called '*a posteriori* knowledge', meaning 'knowledge from the later', because it is knowledge gained from experience.

Plato believed that our knowledge is innate (born within us) and comes *a priori* ('from the earlier') meaning that it exists in us before we gain any sense data from experience. The idea that we can reach knowledge from reason alone, without observation or experience, became the basis for Rationalism, a philosophical approach that directly contradicts Empiricism. Rationalists argue that certain truths exist regardless of our experience of them, and we can access these truths using logic alone. René Descartes (1596–1650) was one such rationalist who argued that universal truths could be found in mathematics and logic and did not require physical evidence.

The Principle of Non-contradiction

The Principle of Non-contradiction is a fundamental element of Aristotle's thought. In *Metaphysics* (Book IV, Part 3), he says: 'The same attribute cannot at the same time belong and not belong to the same subject and in the same respect.' What he is saying here is that contradictory properties – such as the colour red and blue – cannot apply to the same subject at the same time in the same respect. For example, my coat cannot be blue and, at the same time and in the same respect, be red; I can't be standing and sitting at the same time: I am either standing or sitting.

Aristotle says that 'This, then, is the most certain of principles' (*Metaphysics*, IV, 3). It can operate as the anchor that he has been looking for, both for searching out what truly exists, and for knowing what is genuinely true. It can operate as the foundation for knowledge, because it points to that 'which it is impossible to be mistaken' about. Aristotle believes that it is essential for us to find some solid ground (fundamental principles) from which we can begin our reasoning and build knowledge. These principles must not need demonstrating for us to believe they are true;

instead, they must be unequivocally, obviously true. Aristotle believed that non-contradiction was 'more obvious than anything else' (Couvalis, 2009).

However, while it seems easier to accept that a plant cannot be both alive and dead at the same time, or its petals completely red or completely blue, how does this apply to thoughts and beliefs? Aristotle says: in the same way that the same attribute cannot apply to the same thing, in the same respect, at the same time, likewise, 'opposite assertions cannot be true at the same time' (*Metaphysics*, IV, 6). For example, we cannot oppose abortion on the basis that it is always wrong to take a human life and at the same time support the death penalty. Similarly, we cannot say that 'free speech is an inalienable right' and then say that certain people should not be allowed to speak (because their views seem hateful to us, for instance). And yet we find ourselves very often holding contradictory beliefs of all kinds. Aristotle's response was that, although we hold contradictory or inconsistent beliefs, and are able to say these aloud, we don't really believe what we're saying. That is to say, we cannot *rationally* assert two contradictory statements. We know that it is irrational to do so.

How do we justify this principle? We cannot justify it from outside our experience because we use it in our experience, and it is because it is in our experience that we can know the truth of it. Aristotle rejects Plato's argument for *a priori* knowledge because, he says, we cannot stand outside experience and discuss something that has never been in anyone's experience (such as Plato's Forms) because it would be meaningless.

Philosopher Martha Nussbaum (1987) argues that, for Aristotle, science and philosophy are not sharply distinguished and, in every area, he looks to find the basic principles. Aristotle called this *nous* – or 'intellect' – and it is with this faculty, Nussbaum argues, that we grasp first principles; but this is not *a priori*, instead, it is an insight into a fundamental principle through our experience.

What Exists?

Aristotle said that 'being' is always a compound of matter and form (this became known as his theory of Hylomorphism). As we saw in Chapter 2, Plato's forms were separate from the material world. They were immaterial, eternal universals with an existence of their own. Aristotle agreed with Plato that in order to understand the world you must investigate the form, but he took them out of the abstract world and put them in the world around us.

In the first book of the *Physics*, Aristotle introduces us to his ideas of matter and form. He believed that no object is metaphysically simple – all have two unique metaphysical elements: one essence and one matter. The essence is the way of life of the animal or plant, and the matter is the body and all aspects of it. According to Aristotle, matter and essence are not material parts of substances. The matter is formed into the substance it is by the essence that it is. If we think of a plant, such as a rose, the rose is a material substance which has both matter and essence. The essence is the arrangement, nature and state of the rose. This arrangement and order changes as the rose develops from a seed to a bud to the full plant itself. It has an internal process that enables it to gain nutrients from the environment, to process those nutrients and to grow. Each of these processes is part of the plant; you cannot separate the activity of the rose from the actual rose. At all levels, even cellular, each part of the plant is performing the activity needed for that particular plant to develop. The rose's essence determines the properties and activities of every physical part of the rose. In this way, matter is determined by the plant so that particular activities and properties appear. This understanding of essence and matter does not just pertain to plants but to everything in the universe.

So, in contrast to Plato, Aristotle said that the form of something does not exist independently as an entity in itself. It is the pattern or structure of a thing which defines how that thing exists and functions, whether it is human, animal, plant or rock. Without a form, matter would have no properties at all. But, Aristotle argues, something cannot exist if it has no properties; therefore every material thing has to have a form. So, matter is defined by a form to make a substance.

Substances and Accidents

In both *Metaphysics* and *Categories,* Aristotle expands on this idea of substance. For Aristotle, at its very heart, the universe is made up of substances, not particles. This view is clearly very different from the view of modern physics which argues that the universe, fundamentally, consists of elementary particles and forces. Aristotle's reasoning is very difficult to work out but, essentially, he divides the universe into two categories: substances and accidents. 'A substance – that which is called a substance most strictly, primarily, and most of all – is that which is neither said of a subject nor in a subject, e.g. the individual man or individual horse' (*Categories*, 2a13).

The contemporary philosopher, J.L. Ackrill (1981), explains this as follows:

> *'Substances are things: people, objects, planets, chairs, cats, mice. An accident is the feature of the substance. So, a chair is the substance, the fact that it is brown is the accident. You are a substance; the fact that you have red hair, or blue eyes or that you are sitting down or eating a sandwich are all accidents. Substance is the essential nature of something, the thing that defines it.'*

Substances are the fundamental parts of existence because, Aristotle argues, they exist before the existence of accidents; we know about substances before we know about accidents. You cannot have an accident without a substance, but substances can exist without accidents. For example, if we go back to the brown chair: the chair existed before it was covered in brown fabric, but we cannot know brown without knowing the substance. We cannot talk about 'brownness' without talking about brown things.

Another example might be 'a triangle has three sides'. Having three sides is the essential property of what it is to be a triangle, but being an isosceles triangle is a property particular to a type of triangle and so, from the point of view of being a triangle, it is an 'accidental' property. In the same way, being a green triangle or a paper triangle are both incidental to the fundamental essence of being a triangle. There are nine kinds of 'accidents' according to Aristotle: quantity, quality, relation, habit, time, location, situation, action and 'being acted on'. Together with substance, these are the categories that are the basis of Aristotle's ontology (philosophy of the nature of being).

How Can Things Change and be the Same?

In his discussions about substance and form, what Aristotle is really asking are two questions: one about change and one about identity. How can we talk about things that change over time? Given the principle of non-contradiction, how are a caterpillar and a butterfly the same thing?

We experience change all the time, but in order to recognize change and the things that are changing, there must be something that doesn't change, some property within the object that remains fundamentally the same. If we have a block of fresh cheese and we leave it sitting on the side and over time it develops more and more mould until the whole block eventually begins to disintegrate, what are we referring to when we say 'the cheese'? In order to discuss our observations of the cheese, there must be some property that means we can recognize it as the same object so we can coherently discuss its changes. So, the question is, what does not change?

The second question is about identity. Aristotle argues that when we point to something and ask, 'What is it?' what we are really asking is 'Which of the properties in that thing are the fundamental ones, the ones that make it "what it is"?' For example, if I point to you, which of your properties are so fundamental that if they ceased to exist you wouldn't be you? If you changed your hair colour or your jumper, you would still be yourself – but if you ceased to be human or ceased to be flesh and blood, then you would cease to be you.

When an acorn becomes an oak tree, or a human undergoes a process such as death, there must be some matter which persists through the change, according to Aristotle. To say otherwise would be to say that things can come to be out of nothing – and later vanish into nothing. Aristotle agreed with his predecessor, Parmenides, that this is impossible (*Physics*, Book VIII). The properties that are fundamental to an object – to make it be *that object* and no other – are those that remain throughout change. These properties answer the identity (or 'what is it?') question.

The True Nature of Things

Aristotle's view is that we must distinguish between the accidental and essential properties of substance. There is the property that you have brown hair, and this is a property you could lose while still remaining yourself, but you could not lose the property of being human and still be yourself.

Aristotle uses this approach for the whole of reality. As the British philosopher Bryan Magee (1930–2019) explains, we identify things in the world and then add characteristics to them. The fundamental property is what we identify first, such as 'human being', and then we add characteristics, such as 'brown hair'. The subject is the person (human being), the characteristic (which can change) is brown hair. This structure is the basis for the description of the whole world, not only for Aristotle but for all of us. The distinction between the subject and the predicate has become built into our language and our logic. It identifies the fundamental property (the subject of a sentence) clearly; everything else is an accidental property (Magee, 1987).

As Aristotle understood it, the fundamental property is that which persists through all changes, that which sheds attributes and acquires new attributes, in the way that things change shape, colour and position. In this way, Aristotle takes fundamental property to refer to a kind of blueprint for something, on which its identity rests. For instance, look at Socrates, Aristotle says. Socrates cannot consist of the matter that makes up his body, because Socrates' body is changing all the time and will change completely several times over the course of his life, but he is still Socrates.

In *Metaphysics*, Aristotle argues that substance must be a form. A human being can't be matter because matter changes and can be replaced. A further quality of 'substance', according to Aristotle, is that it is 'a this'. Matter is not 'a this' until or unless it has taken on form, just as properties do not exist apart from the substance of which they are a quality. Socrates is 'a this' – he is a substance. If we identified Socrates with the matter of his 10-year-old body, we could not still recognize him as the same person at the age of 40. But if the substance gives us the fundamental 'Socrates', we can recognize him in any shape or age of body. Here, Aristotle is beginning to use the word 'essence' in addition to 'form': 'A given thing seems to be nothing other than its own substance, and something's substance is said to be its essence.' (*Metaphysics*, Book Zeta)

The Ship of Theseus

People are not the only things that we can recognize in this way. For instance, we can replace the parts of a named ship and the same ship still exists. Once we identify the substance, we can then discuss the matter. One very famous example of this argument is a thought experiment known as the 'Ship of Theseus' (or the Theseus Paradox), which was first recorded in written form by the Ancient Greek philosopher Plutarch.

> *'The ship wherein Theseus and the youth of Athens returned from Crete had 30 oars, and was preserved by the Athenians down even to the time of Demetrius Phalereus – for they took away the old planks as they decayed, putting in new and stronger timber in their places, in so much that this ship became a standing example among the philosophers, for the logical question of things that grow; one side holding that the ship remained the same, and the other contending that it was not the same.'* (Plutarch, *Theseus*)

If parts of the ship continue to be replaced, until all of them have been changed, is the Ship of Theseus now a new ship or is it still Theseus' ship? If it is a new ship when all the parts are replaced, then at what point did it become a new ship? And if it is the same ship, what is still the same?

Aristotle would say that it is still the same ship, even after every part has been replaced. He argues that the ship is the same because the 'what it is' to be that ship does not change. This leads us on to another key aspect that underlies Aristotle's philosophy and that is at the heart of most of his ideas: the four causes.

Four Causes

In the *Physics* and *Metaphysics* Aristotle argues that everything has four causes, whether it's an animal, a table or a piece of rock. The four causes together offer a complete explanation of material change in the world, given the principle of non-contradiction and the nature of substances. The four causes are material, formal, efficient and final.

The *Material Cause* answers the question 'what is it made of?' For instance, animals are made of cells, statues are made of marble, and computers are made of electrical components. The material cause tells us something about the properties of the object too, because if made of marble, for example, an item can be carved, or if it is made of cells it might bleed or need oxygen.

The *Formal Cause* is what makes a thing just one thing, rather than many things. The difference between a collection of animal cells, muscle fibre, blood and so on, and a human being, is that a human being has a particular arrangement of these things. The human body is the formal cause, not the different materials from which it is made up. Likewise, the difference between a block of marble and a statue is that the statue has a particular arrangement of parts that makes it a statue as opposed to anything else. The marble could have become flooring or part of a church or temple.

The *Efficient Cause*, or explanation, is the primary source of the change – the person, thing or natural law that causes the thing to come into being or change. This primary source, or efficient cause, might be the sculptor who makes the statue, the mother who gives birth to the child, or the carpenter that makes the table.

The *Final Cause*, or explanation, is perhaps the most important. It is the final purpose for something being the way it is or the reason that it is being done. The purpose of a statue is to be beautiful and/or depict a person or object; a tree grows as it does in order to become a certain type of tree. 'Health' might be the final cause for any number of things, from walking five miles a day, to eating vegan meals or taking medicines. Human beings exist, according to Aristotle, not only to procreate the species but also – because they are rational – they exist to be happy, to achieve eudaimonia and to lead a good life (see Chapter 4).

If we take one object, such as a statue, the four causes are all essential in its coming into existence:

> **The material cause** is the marble (the matter from which it is made).
> **The formal cause** is the shape or form that the sculptor imposes onto the marble.
> **The efficient cause** is the sculptor who brings the statue into existence.
> **The final cause** is the sculptor's purpose for making the sculpture – perhaps to make something beautiful or to create a realistic memento of a particular person.

When thinking about the final cause, Aristotle is using his ideas of teleology: the idea that everything has a goal or purpose. In order to have an explanation of something, he says, we need to understand the end goal – the function of the animal, human or object. Everything in the universe, he says, is aiming to have the best life possible.

From Potential to Actual

Aristotle said that changes which occur over time arise from a potential within the thing, which can turn into a reality (be actualized). He believed that everything contains both potentiality and actuality. Potentiality is the capacity to realize some quality or state if certain conditions are met. If the conditions are right, the potentiality of something becomes actuality (the thing fulfils its potential) – and this is the point at which it achieves its purpose (its final cause). This state of actuality then has the potential to change to a new form of potentiality and then again to actuality in a continuous cycle of change and motion. In *Metaphysics* (Book XII), Aristotle uses the example of 'whiteness'. Something that is 'not white' has the potential to become 'actually white' (to actualize this potential). For example, my house has the potential to be painted blue but now it is in a state of actualized green. If I paint it blue, it will then have the potential to be painted green (or white, red, yellow and so on). This movement from potentiality to actuality led Aristotle to the conclusion that there are stages in causation.

The Prime Mover

In *Metaphysics* Aristotle also identifies three categories of substance, according to whether or not change can occur in their actual or potential being.

Substance Category One contains things or objects that are subject to decay within it. These things are moved by the four causes from a state of potentiality to actuality. My house would be an example of something in Category One as it hasn't always existed in this form, and at some point could be painted or added to or even demolished and re-built.

Substance Category Two involves things that are subject to the four causes and change from potentiality to actuality, but will never decay, die or cease to exist. Aristotle believed that the universe and time exist in this category because of the Greek notion of pre-existing matter. The universe changes and moves from potentiality to actuality but it will not cease to exist.

The final category, Substance Category Three, includes eternal things that are not subject to the four causes. This includes only two things: mathematics (the Greeks believed that mathematics existed in a changeless state awaiting discovery) and something Aristotle called 'the Prime Mover'. It is the Prime Mover that completes Aristotle's understanding of the four causes.

The Prime Mover is the efficient and final cause of the universe. Its 'action' in the universe is passive. The Prime Mover itself exists in a state of 'pure actuality' incapable of change (otherwise it would enter Substance Category Two). This is Aristotle's idea of 'God', but he also refers to the Prime Mover as 'the great attractor'. He claimed that things are attracted towards the perfection found within the Prime Mover's 'pure actuality'. Objects that move from potentiality to actuality fulfil their purpose because their change is brought about through the existence of the Prime Mover.

Aristotle's arguments influenced the thinking of St Thomas Aquinas (in *Summa Theologica* (1485)) and his cosmological argument for the existence of God. For Aquinas, God is the perfection which is found in the actuality. Aquinas, like Aristotle, argued for a first cause of motion and change – an eternal power – which his audience interpreted as 'God'. The Prime Mover, for Aristotle, does not move or have any desire to do so. It is only aware of itself and it attracts everything through its sheer will. It has necessary existence, which means it cannot fail to exist, and it remains in a pure state of actuality because it is perfect. The Prime Mover is the final cause. It has no material, formal or efficient cause; it is the reason the universe is the way that it is. Aristotle is not arguing that the Prime Mover starts off a set of dominoes, that it is a set of causal events in the universe; instead he is focusing on the Prime Mover as the originating cause of all motion that sustains the pattern of change from potentiality to actuality.

Aristotle and Teleology

As we have seen, Aristotle used his argument for teleology in his explanation of the final cause. The Greek word *telos* means 'end' or 'ultimate goal'. Aristotle argued that things change in order to reach their ultimate goal or purpose. Aristotle begins his explanation of living things by identifying its function. We might be able to take apart living things, like plants, animals or humans, and see the parts they consist of, but we will only understand how the parts work when we understand the function of the parts and the living thing itself. The final cause is what makes something the way it is – for humans this is virtue and intelligence, according to Aristotle. Nutrition and reproduction are fundamental to all living things and these are the basic biological explanation of function.

According to Monte Ransome Johnson in *Aristotle on Teleology* (2006), Aristotle normally begins a teleological explanation of a living thing with an identification of its 'good'. What he means by this is 'that at which all things aim' or to put it another way, 'the ultimate end'. So, for example, a human's 'good' would be virtue and happiness (according to Aristotle). An animal's 'good' would be reproduction and survival. Johnson explains that the good of each species is the basis for its explanation. The existence of these goods implies certain requirements or 'hypothetical necessity'. For example, if a fish is to survive and reproduce, it must be able to acquire food, which requires that it move, and so it must have fins, which in turn require tissues, and these must be composed of a certain combination of the elements. Aristotle does not assign human characteristics to animals; for him, the building of a nest by birds or the mating for life of emperor penguins are part of the nature of the animal which needs no rational reflection.

Everything has a Purpose

As we have seen with Aristotle's theories on causation and teleology, he clearly argues that there is a reason for everything. Biological, environmental and anatomical systems have a purpose and so do we. Our purpose, however, is not just procreation and the continuation of our species but, as it is our rationality that sets us apart from other animals, so it is our rationality that is our purpose; by exercising our rationality we will fulfill our nature and lead good lives. The question then becomes 'what is the best life for human beings?' We shall explore this fundamental question in the next chapter.

4. Virtue and Ethics

As we saw in the previous chapter, Aristotle's philosophy rests on the observation and investigation of empirical evidence. This is not only true for ideas about the nature of the world and the cosmos but also true for understanding ethical and political questions. Turning his attention to these kinds of questions, Aristotle writes:

> *'Since, then, the present enquiry does not aim at theoretical knowledge like the others (for we are inquiring not in order to know what virtue is, but in order to become good, since otherwise our inquiry would have been of no use), we must examine the nature of actions, namely how we ought to do them; for these determine also the nature of the states of character that are produced.'* (*Nicomachean Ethics*, Book II, 2)

Aristotle's ethical theory is outlined in his *Nicomachean Ethics* (which may be named in honour of his son or his father, as both were called Nicomachus). Aristotle's ethics rest on some of the ideas that we have already encountered, and which underpin much of his philosophy: function, causation and empirical observation.

The Function Argument

Aristotle looked at nature and considered what humans do differently to other living things. He saw that we do everything plants and other animals do, but that we also have the capacity to reason, unlike any other living things. As we know, Aristotle believed that any intentional act that a person does has a purpose (*telos*) and a higher aim. For example, you are reading and learning about Aristotle and his philosophy with the aim of understanding his ideas. The final aim of life will be different for everyone, but every rational activity you engage in has a purpose leading to an aim. As explained in Chapter 3, Aristotle described this as 'the good'. He saw this as a combination of what is good for yourself and what is good for everyone. For Aristotle, everything has a function, task or work (*ergon*) that it needs to do. For humans, 'being good' is to perform your function well. The purpose of human action is happiness, Aristotle claimed, and so you are being good when you are happy (because you are performing your function well). So, we achieve our ultimate good (eudaimonia) when we act rationally in accordance with the virtues (function) in order to achieve eudaimonia (aim).

Aristotle believed that the distinctive end purpose of human beings is to be rational. This might seem straightforward, but it is made more complex because of the significance of *ergon* (which here means putting reason into practice). This is where virtue ethics comes into its own. Through the practice of *arête* (excellence or virtue) reason becomes an activity of the soul, leading to *eudaimonia* (translated as 'human flourishing' or 'happiness'). True happiness is the process of flourishing, the joy of being what you are meant to be and doing what you are meant to do.

However, Aristotle assumes that everything has a function; because his observations lead him to conclude that some things have a purpose, he assumes that all things have a purpose. Just because your eye has a function, your stomach has a function, your liver, feet and skin have a function, does this mean that you, as a whole person, have a function? This question has tormented philosophers through the ages, with Existentialists like Jean-Paul Sartre (1905–80) saying that it is precisely our lack of function that gives us freedom. Sartre believed that 'existence precedes essence' (we are born and then find a purpose), but Aristotle believed that a purpose exists for human beings before any of us are born, and that is eudaimonia.

Achieving Eudaimonia

Eudaimonia is a difficult word to translate from the Greek. It can be translated as happiness, but Aristotle had a different understanding of happiness to us. He was not talking about a state of mind, or psychological happiness, but a way of living – something active. A more accurate translation may be 'flourishing' – living in a way that feels enlivening and good to us. The question of what a 'good life' is was not a theoretical enquiry for Aristotle; he wanted to work out what was 'good' for human beings so that we would have a better understanding of how to live our lives in a full, purposeful and enjoyable way. At the same time, he saw eudaimonia as objective; it is something that we can make a judgement on – we know at the end of our lives if we achieved it. It is a judgement we make about the whole life, as to whether it was a life lived well, rather than focusing on moments of happiness.

Aristotle saw eudaimonia as the goal in life but made it clear that it should not be equated with the idea of pleasure. He believed that the value of pleasure is determined by the value of the activity you are performing. If we take pleasure in good activities, the pleasure is good; if we take pleasure in bad activities, the pleasure is bad. He argued that every creature aims at pleasure, but this is not our only purpose because we also seek out other things (such as having friends, being healthy, and so on) and even things that may not necessarily bring us pleasure, such as being virtuous or courageous. Living the good life might bring pleasure but this is not why we seek it. Aristotle was looking for the highest good; all the other goals we have – such as health, wealth and love – are sought by us because they promote wellbeing or flourishing, not because one of them alone is where flourishing resides.

One obvious question is this: How far through our life do we have to get before we achieve eudaimonia? The answer is that eudaimonia is about living virtuously, dealing with good and bad events as best as we can, while continuing to develop our virtues. Someone has attained eudaimonia if they are living the 'good life'.

Intellectual and Moral Virtues

In order to achieve a good life, we will need to use our power of rationality to live well. Or to put it another way, reasoning fully over the course of our lives is how we will flourish. How do we know if we are applying our reasoning well? We make sure that we are doing it with *arête* – meaning both 'virtue' and 'excellence'. 'Virtue' here is virtue in the sense of the characteristics, traits or dispositions of persons or things that make them successful. These virtues are part of our purpose and help us fulfil our function; for example, sharpness is a virtue in knives, courage is a virtue in a soldier. Virtues need to be refined and honed; they are both part of the means of reaching the end product and part of the end product itself; they are activities that make a thing 'good'. Virtuous activity will enable us to live the good life and experience eudaimonia.

In this sense, living well consists in exercising certain skills that we recognize as 'virtues', such as being courageous, just, friendly and generous. Character traits such as these can be practised so that they become a way of being. Our resulting behaviour, as a consequence, will affect the way we live, both from day to day and over the course of a lifetime.

It is important to note that Aristotle sees virtues as good habits that we will need to (and can) acquire, and which regulate our emotions. For example, in response to my natural feelings of fear, I should develop the virtue of courage, which allows me to be firm when facing danger. Julia Annas (2006) adds to this definition and points out that virtues are not a mindless habit but a disposition to behave in a certain way and not others. It is developed by making conscious, skillful choices, rather than heedless, habitual ones. (In this sense Aristotle's idea of the 'good life' closely resembles Buddhist ideas of living 'skillfully', consciously and well.)

Aristotle considers qualities that enable people to live together to be the best; only when those qualities are displayed can we really flourish, because they are necessary for our development as social beings. So, developing virtues is a necessary feature of living alongside others; it is a social, political and moral feature of life, not just a personal one.

Types of Virtues

Aristotle divides virtues into two types: intellectual and moral. Intellectual virtues are those that pertain to the part of the soul that engages in reasoning, and moral virtues are those that pertain to the part of the soul that cannot itself reason but is capable of following reasoning.

Intellectual Virtues

These are the virtues of the mind, such as the ability to understand, reason and make sound judgements. These are in turn divided into two kinds: those involved in theoretical reasoning (such as theoretical wisdom) and those involved in practical thinking (such as practical wisdom). Through teaching in childhood, we first learn theoretical reasoning, and once we can think well logically, we can develop practical wisdom.

Moral Virtues

These are the ethical virtues, or virtues of character. They are not innate but are acquired through repetition and practice, like learning a musical instrument, and they are only fully developed when combined with practical wisdom. The more independent we become, and the more capable of thinking for ourselves, the more our skills will improve, and our emotional characteristics and responses will become finely honed. It is through the practice of these ethical virtues that one becomes a particular type of person.

According to Aristotle, we are born without character. This develops over time, through education and lived experience, and it is shaped and moulded through practice. In the same way that we might enjoy perfecting our skills in playing sports or musical instruments, the virtuous person takes pleasure in practising and exercising her or his intellectual and ethical skills. Aristotle suggests that it will take many years to develop a good character because it is a practical discipline.

A Question of Emotion

One question levelled at Aristotle is 'Where does emotion fit into this?' Can personal emotions be part of practical wisdom or do emotions lead to poor judgement? Aristotle recognizes the problem of emotions, particularly at the start of the journey to eudaimonia. This is a lifetime's work: 'For one swallow does not make a summer, nor does one day; and so too one day, or a short time, does not make a man blessed and happy' (*Nicomachean Ethics*, Book I). Phronesis (practical wisdom) is acquired through experience and past judgements, and so we will choose to act justly for its own sake, because it will lead to justice (not because we feel emotionally inclined one way or the other).

It is a mature will that enables a person to act with wisdom. Thinking about virtues, Annas (2006) argues, leads to thinking about one's life as a whole. This, she says, is crucial because the virtues only make sense when we think of our life as part of a unity. Cultivating the virtues is worthwhile because it will mean that we will live our life well as a whole. Our final end – eudaimonia – is not about things like money or fame; it is about living in a certain way and pursuing that actively.

Voluntary and Involuntary Actions

It is important to remember that virtue theory is about choice. For Aristotle there is a difference between voluntary, involuntary and non-voluntary actions and he discusses this in Book III of the *Ethics*. Moral responsibility is about voluntary action. When we act voluntarily, we know what we are doing, when we act involuntarily, we do so because of ignorance or because we are the subject of force. For example, if I bump into someone this is involuntary, but if I deliberately push them then that is a voluntary action that I have chosen to do. Sometimes we might act voluntarily but not necessarily from choice. It could be argued that the actions of children are often voluntary (such as snatching another child's toy) but not chosen, because they have not deliberated about it. An action is involuntary when it is done under compulsion and causes pain to the person acting. If an action is done in ignorance, it may be called involuntary if the person later recognizes his ignorance, but it will be a non-voluntary action if the person does not recognize their ignorance or doesn't suffer from ignorance. If an adult helps themselves to someone else's belongings and is either suffering from ignorance or doesn't realize that they are ignorant, this also is considered a non-voluntary action.

For Aristotle choice is about deliberation: reasoned thought about how to achieve an end. The point for virtue theory is that the virtuous person *chooses* to act virtuously. Their behaviour is not accidental. At the beginning of the journey to eudaimonia we choose voluntarily to develop the right character traits. As the journey continues and we develop these traits, our choice becomes less 'voluntary' as we become the sort of person who makes the right choices as a matter of course. This is because we have developed the right character. For Aristotle we are morally responsible for our choices. If someone has become bad it is because they chose to do bad things at the beginning of their life and have developed bad character traits. In this way we are partly responsible for the traits we develop.

Virtue in Slaves and Women

It should be noted that Aristotle said all free males are born with the potential to become ethically virtuous and wise in both theoretical and practical ways. Women and slaves were not considered capable of achieving this kind of life. This is partly due to the paradigm in which Aristotle lived (Greek 'democracy' only acknowledged free men as citizens) and largely because the teaching required to gain the virtuous skills was not given to slaves or women, so they could not reach the same level of intellectual and ethical development – at least in the way that Aristotle envisaged. In addition, it was only through the productive labour of women and slaves that free men were liberated to pursue intellectual lifestyles and activities. In the *Politics*, Aristotle raises a question about the morality of slavery, which would have been considered irrelevant and odd at the time as slavery was considered a normal part of civic society. Unfortunately, Aristotle also saw it as essential to the functioning of Athenian society and believed that it was for the good of both masters and slaves, because he saw slaves as lacking rational capacity and capable of only manual labour. He regarded them as incapable of governing their own lives and were therefore the benefactors of other people telling them what to do. However, having drawn this distinction between two types of people – those equipped to command and those who preferred to obey direction – in Book VI of the *Politics* he argues that it is impossible to know who these people are. How do we know who is 'naturally' suited to give or receive orders? Slaves in Ancient Greece were either born into slavery or were prisoners of war. Neither condition necessitated a particular set of traits or abilities, Aristotle says, pointing to a problem in assuming that slavery was automatically just. Although Aristotle believed that there were natural slaves whose relationship with their master was harmonious, he did question the idea of people defined as slaves by law due to some misfortune (for example, by being captured in war). In a case such as this, Aristotle deemed the relationship between slave and master to be unnatural. Aristotle himself had slaves but granted them freedom in his will.

Aristotle's position on women was similar to that of slaves. In Chapter 12 of the *Politics* he says that 'the relation of male to female is by nature a relation of superior to inferior and ruler to ruled'. The reason given is the same: 'The slave is wholly lacking the deliberative element; the female has it, but it lacks authority; the child has it, but it is incomplete'. It is unclear what Aristotle meant by 'lacks authority'. It could be that he was referring to their physical inferiority which meant they were unable to enforce their will, or that they were ruled more by emotion than reason, and therefore lacked the authority of logical reasoning. In any case, for both women and slaves in Ancient Greece, education was withheld, as was access to public life (including politics). By denying the development and practice of skills that Aristotle himself saw as required learning, slaves and women were effectively prevented from gaining knowledge – and this lack of knowledge was then used against them as 'proof' of their poorer intellectual and ethical capabilities.

Aristotle's teachings on the issue of slavery and women make for uncomfortable reading today. While we can point to the fact that he was writing in a classical political context where slavery was part of the state, what is more problematic is the way his writings provided the intellectual case for slavery from antiquity. The Spanish and Portuguese conquest of South America with its system of *encomienda* and the slave trade from Africa to North America which treated slaves as chattels found its academic justification in Aristotle and its theological justification in the Bible.

However, his teachings also provided some enlightenment. Aquinas took up his definition of man as a 'rational animal' and thought that this capacity was more widely distributed through humanity than Aristotle had argued. A follower of Aquinas, and therefore Aristotle to an extent, Bartolome de las Casas (1484-1556) championed the cause of the rights of native peoples in the Americas, particularly in Mexico. Aristotle's legacy on the issue of slavery is a mixed one but it should be acknowledged that because his analysis of human nature claimed to be based on empirical observation it gave it a scientific authenticity that was used by later scholars to make the case that the rational capacity was not evenly distributed.

The Doctrine of the Mean

Aristotle argued that it is important to strike a balance (mean or golden mean) between extremes, as it is this balance that leads to virtue. In mathematics, the mean is the average, so if we have a list of 10 numbers, we add them up and divide by 10 (by the amount of numbers there are) and this gives us the mean.

Aristotle, however, doesn't quite use the term in the same way as we do in maths. He argues that while the mean is the average or the balance between two things, it is relative to us individually. So, my mean, or average of wisdom, will not be the same as yours. Aristotle explains that this understanding is crucial to our ideas of virtue:

> *'Virtue, then, is a state of character concerned with choice, lying in a mean, i.e. the mean relative to us, this being determined by a rational principle, and by that principle by which the man of practical wisdom would determine it.'* (*Nicomachean Ethics*, Book II)

Developing virtues is not about being the best, but about acting between excess and deficiency. It is about choosing the right way to act with the appropriate degree of love, honesty, and so on, in the circumstances. So, we might be angry if someone steals our car but irritated when we have misplaced the car keys. The mean depends on the circumstances and the person. What is courage for me may be rashness for someone else. We have to apply phronesis to decide on the right course of action.

One way of thinking about virtues is as character traits. We do not want to be the person who is fearful all the time nor the person who is not afraid enough; we want to be the person who knows when to be courageous and when to be cautious, when to feel fear and when not to. We want to understand what the 'intermediate' stage is between the virtues and vices so we can act appropriately.

One of the key strengths of virtue theory is that it focuses on the growth of the moral agent rather than on the act itself. It starts from the point of thinking about your life as a whole. It shouldn't and doesn't seek to tell you what to do; it is not a formula for action. Its desirable ethical condition is about having the best character. This gives it a flexibility that is often lacking in other ethical theories which prescribe a course of action according to rules. Virtue ethics can help in making decisions. You do not just learn what the right thing to do is but also why they are the right things to do, and so you gain an understanding of why you are acting as you are.

Aristotle's vision is the cultivation of the whole person, including reason and emotion, in order to overcome the weakness of will through practical wisdom. He recognized that life is in a constant state of flux, and that it is through working towards practical wisdom that someone can develop a moral education, create a consistent character and the ability to know how to act in every situation.

Problems with Aristotle's Ethical Arguments

The flexibility of Aristotle's ethics may be a strength in some ways, but it also creates problems. If faced with two potentially virtuous acts, we might not be able to decide what to do. Aristotle argues that without a good character we cannot understand what good is, but this means that knowledge of 'what is good' cannot be obtained by everyone: it can only be obtained by those who have already achieved virtue. But if you are a rational being surely you should be able to understand right and wrong and access the good?

The other key problem is that definitions of virtue will differ from community to community, and therefore decisions, too, will differ from community to community. While this may seem a sensible alternative to set rules, it would allow for different communities to act in a variety of ways. The virtues prized by Aristotle and his peers might not necessarily be the same today. This cultural relativism means that virtue theory could condone unjust acts such as slavery, which was acceptable in Aristotle's society and might be acceptable in some societies today, though totally unacceptable to most modern thinkers.

In the final chapter of the *Ethics*, Aristotle tells us that his project is not yet complete. We can only make human beings virtuous if we create the environment in which they can flourish. Humans cannot achieve eudaimonia unless they live in communities that foster the good habits and virtues needed to create a good life. Therefore, Aristotle says, we must investigate the different political systems in the Greek cities and find the best political order for creating an environment conducive to eudaimonia.

Ethics and politics are both practical sciences which address our daily needs as human beings. As with the *Ethics*, Aristotle wants to create the kind of people who, when confronted with political decisions, will know the right thing to do, when to follow the rules, and when to deviate from them. Again, the idea of *telos* links both ethics and politics together. Just as a plant can only fulfil its *telos* with the right soil, water and sunlight, so a person can only fulfil their *telos* in a well-organized political system.

5. The Soul

Aristotle's investigation on the soul (psyche) is often called his investigation into psychology but, compared to modern psychology, Aristotle's investigations are much broader in scope. He includes a discussion on the nature of life itself, comprising animals as well as plants.

The soul is central to Aristotle's theory of life. It is the element that connects his ethics, politics, natural sciences and metaphysics. He argues that understanding the nature of the soul is crucial to comprehending the principles that govern all animal life. In his major treatise, *On the Soul* (*De Anima*) Aristotle sought to 'grasp and understand, first its essential nature, and secondly its properties'. He admits that 'one of the most difficult things in the world' is to define the soul and to which class it belongs. It is important to note that, although we translate psyche as 'soul', Aristotle means 'soul' as something that animates a living thing, that gives it life. In Aristotle's time there was much debate as to whether the soul exists independently of the body or as an equal part of it, or whether it is dependent on the body for its survival. Aristotle argues that the soul is part of the physical body and this sets him apart from the pre-Socratics and Plato. In Part II of *On the Soul*, Aristotle looked at his predecessors' arguments in a bid to 'profit by whatever is sound in their suggestions and avoid their error'. Let us first look, then, at how Plato defined the soul.

Plato's Theory on the Soul

Plato had a very different way of thinking about humans and living things. He argued that humans could be broken down into three parts: the body, the mind and the soul. The body is the physical part that is only concerned with the material world, and through which we experience the world we live in. The mind, which is directed towards the heavenly realm of ideas, is immortal. It is with our minds that we understand the eternal world of the Forms (see Chapter 2). The soul is the driving force of the body, it is what gives us our identity.

Plato's claims about the soul are found in his works the *Phaedo* and the *Republic*. In this latter work, he divides the soul into three parts: reason, spirit and appetite. Reason is the senior partner and works through logic and knowledge. Spirit is aligned with reason and controls emotion, motivation, and ambition, while appetite is about desire. It is the disharmony between these three parts that lead to sin. In the *Phaedo*, Plato gives us four different reasons for the soul's existence and for its immortality: The Argument from Opposites, The Theory of Recollection, The Argument from Affinity, and The Argument from the Form of Life.

The first argument, The Argument from Opposites, argues that everything comes to be from out of its opposite. For example, if life and death are opposites and death comes out of life, then life must come out of death. So we can reason that as the living become dead, so the dead must become living and therefore the soul must be immortal because it is locked in a cycle of life and death.

His second argument, The Theory of Recollection, suggests that learning is a process of remembering things one knows before birth. The soul exists before birth, Plato says, existing in the world of the Forms where it is filled with knowledge. This means that the soul must be eternal.

The Argument from Affinity concludes that the soul is eternal because it is a non-perceptible and intelligible thing, like the Forms, rather than a material object which can be destroyed.

His final proof is The Argument from the Form of Life. As all things partake in their Forms (e.g. green things partake in the Form of Green or chairs partake in the Form of Chair), and as the soul participates in the Form of Life, it must be eternal.

Aristotle's Theory on the Soul

Aristotle disagreed with Plato and instead divided the soul into two parts: first the Rational (which was further divided into the scientific part which looks for truth, and the calculative part which is the decision-making part). Second, the Irrational which again was divided into two: desire (what one wants to do); and basic desire (the vegetative part, for example the desire for food or sex). But, more importantly for Aristotle, the body and soul are not two separate substances, as Plato argues, but are one thing. Souls are not immaterial, spiritual things that exist within a body, rather they are facilities or capabilities. Aristotle tries to explain his understanding of the distinction between the body and the soul by using the analogy of an axe. If an axe were a living thing then its body would be made of wood and metal. However, its soul would be the thing which made it an axe, i.e. its capacity to chop: 'if an axe had a soul that soul would be cutting'.

If it lost its ability to chop it would cease to be an axe – it would simply be wood and metal. What is important for Aristotle is the end purpose of something: an axe chops, an eye sees, an animal is animated in the sense that it lives, with different animals having different ultimate purposes, etc. This is what is meant by 'teleology' from the Greek *telos*, meaning end. We can see this idea of *telos* in much of Aristotle's work, particularly in the *Ethics* and in cosmology. The function argument is an important aspect of Virtue Theory: man should fulfill his function which is to live the good life (see Chapter 4). In other words, he should engage in rational activity which is the function of all humans.

Aristotle dismisses Plato's argument for the Forms which, as we saw in Chapter 2, theorizes that true reality exists beyond normal perceptions of the world and that what we perceive around us is but a shadow of this truth. For Aristotle, there is no clear evidence for this. Instead he appeals to our senses, claiming that it is through them that we experience reality. Aristotle saw our world and our lives as final; he did not believe in an afterlife as such, although in *On the Soul* he does suggest that the 'active intellect' does not perish. Although Aristotle believed in a supernatural Prime Mover (see Chapter 3), this being has no direct interaction with our world and gives no evidence for a life beyond death. The soul, however, is a central notion to his theory of life, although the word 'psyche' means something different to us and we attach different ideas to the word dependent on our upbringing. In *On the Soul*, he argues that the soul is a system of interrelated parts that keeps an animal alive. It is immaterial and develops when a creature develops, and when the creature dies then it dies also. The soul is the form of the animal. It's not something independent of itself; it is a set of capacities that make it what it is – what it can do. For something to have a soul it needs to have a functioning, organic body.

Discussing Aristotle's method of biological investigation on BBC Radio 4 in 2019, British lecturer in Ancient Philosophy, Sophia Connell, suggests that the soul is responsible for nutrition, temperature regulation, cognition etc. Each animal's body, she says, is suitable for its soul, meaning that transmigration of the soul is not feasible; you can't have a dog's soul enter a cat's body because the dog's soul is not in the form of a cat. The soul provides knowledge to the natural body. In humans, it provides reasoning, desire, locomotion, perception and comprehension. The body and soul – matter and form – work together to give life. Anything that nourishes itself, that grows, decays, moves about (on its own, not just when moved by something else), perceives, or thinks, is alive. And the soul is what is causally responsible for the animate behaviour (the life activities) of a living thing.

Classes of the Soul

In his work, *On the Soul*, Aristotle embeds an understanding of the soul in an understanding of nature and animal life, using the method he has used in his classification of animals. First, he says, we must define what class or family the soul belongs to. Aristotle argues that there are three degrees of the soul:

Nutritive Soul

The most basic level of the soul, which all forms of life possess and are animated by, is a nutritive soul. This incites all living things to feed themselves and to reproduce in order to keep the cycle of life going. Aristotle sees this type of soul as being particular to plants.

Sensitive Soul

Animals, as living things, possess a nutritive soul, but are set apart from plant life by reason of their possessing senses, which plants do not. All animals are able to perceive objects in nature by using at least one of their senses. In this way, animals are able to feel pleasure and pain, feel desire, and even possess a basic kind of memory and imagination. Aristotle calls this the sensitive soul.

Rational Soul

Human beings, however, possess both the nutritive soul and the sensitive soul, and they have the highest level of soul by virtue of their ability to reason. Aristotle calls this the rational soul, which he sees as being singular to humans. He explains this element of the soul by marking out an important difference between perception (which animals possess) and thinking (which only humans can do). Perception, Aristotle argues, depends upon an object, which an animal then discerns through one or more of their senses. Thinking, however, does not depend upon an object. Through their ability to reason, humans use imagination, judgement and analysis to think. They can do this whether an object is there in front of them or not, something animals cannot do.

Actuality and Potentiality

In Book II of *On the Soul*, Aristotle defines the soul by using the definitions of actuality and potentiality, which we looked at in Chapter 3. He describes it as the 'first grade of actuality of a natural body having life potentially in it'. But what does he mean by this? Let's go back to the metaphor of the axe.

The axe has been made by moving raw materials and manipulating them into a form for a specific purpose. We can look at the creation of the axe as a movement from the potential to the actual: it began as wood and metal, which had the potential to become an axe; these materials were then moved from a state of potentiality to a state of actually being an axe. But whereas an axe is an artificial thing, which has its form imposed on it from the outside, things in nature, such as plants, animals and humans, have their form imposed on them from the inside. So if we think of the body as matter (raw materials) and the soul as the form, it is the soul that has made the body what it is – a functioning, living thing with the ability to eat, recreate, move, perceive and think.

The Thinking Part of the Soul

Aristotle also applied his distinction of actuality and potentiality to the human ability to think. For him, actual knowledge is associated with objects that exist in the world, and potential knowledge uses imagination or experience to understand what has the potential to exist but may not yet. However, as potential knowledge doesn't use the senses directly (none of the five senses are used to think), it means that this aspect of the soul can exist without a body. Aristotle concludes then, that this part of the soul is eternal.

Aristotle's concept of the human soul is more psychological in nature than spiritual, however. When describing part of the soul as being eternal, he is not referring to the afterlife, as many religious doctrines are when speaking of the soul. For Aristotle, the soul is the source of thought and the drive behind movement. But his claim that the thinking part of the soul is eternal creates a contradiction in his thinking, as he claims that the soul cannot exist without the body. This makes it somewhat problematic.

The Unity of Soul and Body

Despite Aristotle's belief that 'thought alone comes in from outside, and that it alone is divine; for corporeal actuality has no connection at all with the actuality of thought', he believed that every other aspect of the soul is not separable from the body. As we have seen, he regarded the body as the material object, and the soul as the form of the body, and therefore not capable of existing without the body. For Aristotle, soul has little to do with personal identity and individuality. There is no reason to think that one (human) soul is in any important respect different from any other (human) soul. The form of one human being is the same as the form of any other. You and I have different souls because we are different people. But we are different human beings because we are different compounds of form and matter. That is, different bodies are both animated by the same set of capacities, by the same (kind of) soul.

This idea is completely at odds with Plato, as we saw at the beginning of this chapter. There are two dominant schools of thought in the West regarding the body and the soul. Those that follow Plato's line of thought are referred to as Dualists. René Descartes, the seventeenth century French philosopher, embraced the dualism of mind and body in much of his theoretical works. Many religions believe in the distinction between body and soul: Hinduism teaches that the soul survives the death of the body through reincarnation but in another form such as an animal or another person. Dualism is the argument that body and soul (mind) are separate substances that exist independently from each other. The theory has been tremendously influential in the philosophy of mind.

The alternative position, that of materialism (or physicalism), is more along the lines of Aristotle's thinking (although his approach was not in any modern – or ancient – sense materialist). Materialism argues that there is no mind (soul) without body and some even argue that there is no 'mind' at all, there is only the physical brain. Mental events may not look like physical events, but ultimately that is exactly what they are. For example, when we boil a kettle, the water in the kettle is liquid but the steam which comes out of the spout is not. If we did not know what steam was, we would think it was a different substance from the water. However, steam is nothing but water in gaseous form. Everything, some materialists argue, can be reduced to the physical; art is just paint on a canvas; music is sound waves; and emotions are just psychochemical reactions in the brain.

However, while Aristotle's thinking can be seen in materialist theory, he doesn't go as far as to reduce the soul (mind) to just the physical. In *On the Soul*, he does make a distinction between two kinds of mind; one passive, and one active. Although there have been varying interpretations of this passage, one reading is that Aristotle argues that there is an active mind which forms concepts and a passive mind which stores all the ideas and beliefs. In other passages, Aristotle speaks of the soul as being located in the heart and explains mental states in reference to changes in the sense organs, which would suggest that, on the whole, Aristotle was a materialist.

In the end, though, we should probably see Aristotle as steering some kind of middle course between Plato's dualist ideas and modern ideas of materialism. For Aristotle, it is the form and matter of the soul which are important, and which makes the living thing what it is. Form and matter are inextricably linked, not only in biology and zoology, but in all of Aristotle's investigations. Even in the *Poetics* and *Rhetoric* we see Aristotle's fundamental principles: the relationship between form and matter; the idea of teleology; everything has a purpose and in achieving that purpose the plant, animal, person, or object is able to lead the best life it can.

6. Rhetoric and Poetics

The *Poetics* is, as far as we know, the world's first work of literary theory. But why did Aristotle write a book about literature? Literature and poetry were very important in Greek culture, not only as a source of pleasure but also as sources of moral and practical instruction. Aristotle wanted to help poets write better poetry and enable people to increase their pleasure and understanding of the plays and epics that the Greek audiences enjoyed.

The *Poetics* is divided into 26 chapters, which mainly focus on tragedy as a case study for demonstrating some of Aristotle's ideas. He examines drama and epic poetry (lengthy narrative poetry), and how they achieve their effects, and he analyzes tragedy and the ways in which it plays on our emotions. Aristotle particularly admired Sophocles (c. 497–406 BCE) and was a huge fan of the play *Oedipus Rex*, which he uses as an example throughout the *Poetics*. *Oedipus Rex* (*Oidipous Tyrannos* in Greek) is probably the most well-known Greek tragedy to modern readers. It tells the story of a man called Oedipus who has become king of Thebes by, unknowingly, killing his father (Laius) and marrying his mother (Jocasta). *Oedipus Rex* is the second play in the trilogy, during which Oedipus tries to find Laius' murderer which, of course, is himself. The play ends in extreme tragedy with Jocasta hanging herself and Oedipus gouging out his own eyes. Greek tragedy followed a set of conventions: each play begins with a prologue where the background to the story is explained, then the main characters enter and the story continues over three or four episodes, with breaks for songs that allow the chorus to comment on the story.

The *Poetics*, along with many of Aristotle's works, was translated by medieval Arab scholars and effectively saved by them for posterity. Their translations eventually made their way back to Europe, and during the Renaissance the *Poetics* became a playwriting manual for many dramatists of the era. It continues to be a standard text for would-be Hollywood screenwriters today, many of whom use Aristotle's storytelling techniques to help create plots and character arcs for films.

A Dangerous Art

The *Poetics* is Aristotle's answer to Plato's writings on poetry. Although, as Stephen Halliwell (1998) points out, Aristotle never mentions Plato in the *Poetics*, he uses it to address his mentor's concerns over the art form. While Plato was attracted to poetry, he also thought it was dangerous because it so intensely affects our souls when we are experiencing it. He argued that it arouses intense emotions and can overcome rationality. (This seems exaggerated but – to give a modern-day equivalent – if you think of your favourite song and the emotions it arouses in you, perhaps Plato has a point!) Plato believed that we can be blinded by the power of poetry to act irrationally, swept along by a tide of emotion, which is the antithesis of how Plato believed we should live.

Plato was also concerned with what sort of images of the world poetry gives us, as it can create entirely fictional and fantastic worlds that are unrealistic and false. He was also worried about the credentials of the poets themselves and how they were revered by society. In the same way that today some people are concerned about the influence of modern-day celebrities, Plato worried that the poets could have an influence on the impressionable and young. One need only think of the romantic poets of early nineteenth-century Europe – such as Byron, Shelley and Coleridge, who were famous for their radical views, drinking and drug taking – or songwriters, playwrights, rock musicians and rap musicians who have been routinely accused (unfairly) of glorifying alcohol, drug use, gang affiliation and radicalism, to see Plato's point. Poetry and drama do seem to bring with them false realities and untamed emotions. Plato argued that playwrights should submit their work to the state for approval before it could be performed.

Aristotle attempts to show Plato another way of looking at poetry, as an art form which deserves respect and is naturally independent and exploratory. Nick Lowe (2000) suggests that the opening chapters of the *Poetics* are trying to propose a kit for playwriting and storytelling: the way it acts as a guide continues to make it popular today.

In the case of drama, Aristotle's words in the *Poetics* have set the standard, to the extent that, in the Western world, there has not been any theory of drama, or discussion of its structure and inner workings, without reference to Aristotle. Published in Europe around 1500, the *Poetics* became the centre of debate and discussion. Aristotle asks a fundamental question: if we know art is an imitation, then why are we still moved by it?

Aristotle believed that we are naturally attracted to poetry and art. He observed that imitations of things have the power to fascinate and enthrall us, while the real thing might in fact leave us disgusted. We can also learn from art; it has the power to inspire feelings, states of mind and awareness of abstract, general ideas. To Aristotle, the emotive arousal, the acts of catharsis, the release of sentimental tensions are good for us. In the *Poetics,* Aristotle identified the patterns and themes that made for successful drama. His theory of what makes a good story is still used by storytellers today.

Tragedy as the Highest Form of Art

Where Plato thought that tragedy was dangerous and should be censored, Aristotle argued that it is the highest form of art. While it is a form of imitation, like all poetry, and therefore does not show the 'real world', it still has a serious purpose: to show things as they could be and not as they are. Because of this, Aristotle argued, poetry is a more philosophical and noble discipline than history, which just records events. While Plato feared the moral ambiguity of tragedy, Aristotle placed it at the centre of an art form that targets pity and fear. All art forms, Aristotle and Plato agree, are mimesis (they create images of things). However, Plato had failed to acknowledge that art and literature are more than just copies: they have a purpose. The artist idealizes the world and creates an image with its own beauty and meaning; a poet creates something more than reality through his interpretation and perception of the object. The artistic creation leads us to the essential reality of life rather than taking us away from the truth.

Plato dismissed poetry and tragedy because they do not teach morality, but Aristotle asked about the function of art: Is the purpose of the artist or writer to teach something, or to communicate an experience, produce something of beauty, or express the emotions of life?

Aristotle does agree with Plato when he calls the poet an imitator. The poet and artist imitate what is past or present, what is believed, and what is ideal. But Aristotle believed that humans are born naturally imitative and this is how we develop our character; we can see this idea in both the *Politics* and the *Ethics*, where Aristotle is concerned that we create role models. Because we have a fundamental desire to know and understand, we take great pleasure in imitation. For example, we take pleasure in a great painting or piece of poetry. Poetry does not make people weaker or too sentimental – instead it ennobles them. David Daiches (1981) summarizes Aristotle's views thus: 'Tragedy (Art) gives new knowledge, yields aesthetic satisfaction and produces a better state of mind.'

Renewal Through Catharsis

Catharsis is a purging of emotion through art forms. When we look at a work of art, or watch a play or film, or read a book, our emotions are aroused, and this brings about a release of tension. Art in all its forms allows our deep complex emotions a means of expression and in doing so brings about spiritual renewal. Plato argued that tragedy cannot teach us anything, but Aristotle disagreed, saying that by arousing pity and fear, tragedy does something beneficial; the experience of intense emotion allows you to re-balance your emotional capacities and gain knowledge from the experience. Both Plato and Aristotle agreed that watching a great tragedy will bring out strong emotions, but Plato is fearful that these emotions remain with us and leave us in an irrational emotional state, whereas Aristotle thought it was possible to move into a restored equilibrium through catharsis. This means that we can learn from the experience and apply what we have learnt to our own lives and our own understanding of ethics and virtue.

How are we to provoke such intense feelings in the audience? Aristotle suggests that the core elements of a plot should be reversal (*peripeteia*) and recognition (*anagnorisis*), and through these, fear and pity will be aroused.

Reversal (*Peripeteia*)

Reversal is defined in the *Poetics* as 'a change by which the action veers round to its opposite, subject always to our rule of probability or necessity' (the rule being how likely a character is to react to a given situation because of human nature, either because it is what most people would do (probability) or because of what we might be 'forced' to do (necessity)); it is literally a reversal of fortune. Just when we think that the protagonist of the story is about to win, something negative happens. Aristotle thought it was the most important and powerful element in tragedy.

Aristotle's idea of reversal has had a huge impact on both ancient and modern literature and particularly modern film-making. Aristotle used Sophocles' tragedy *Oedipus Rex* as his example to explain this, but there are plenty of modern examples that we can use to show the importance of reversal.

For example, (spoiler alert!) at the end of the movie *The Empire Strikes Back* (1980), Luke and his friends escape from the Empire, but it is at the expense of Luke's hand, which Darth Vader cuts off during their fight, and the revelation by Darth Vader that he is Luke's father, which devastates Luke. The thriller *Seven* (1997) is another good example. Two detectives, David Mills and William Somerset, are hunting a serial killer who uses the seven deadly sins to symbolize each victim. Just when we think John Doe, the killer, is about to give up the location of his two final victims and make a confession there is a shocking twist which elevates the tragedy and defines the film.

There are many examples of reversal of fortune, and the more shocking and devastating the better, according to Aristotle. The reversal should have a profound impact on the central character and, therefore, on the audience. Both reversal and recognition happen suddenly, but Aristotle does not think they should be used just for the sake of it, but because they show the limit of human agency. They show that human beings move through the world trying to bring about certain goals and ends, but are always at the mercy of their environment, and the techniques of reversal and recognition show the limits of humans' ability to control their lives.

Recognition (*Anagnorisis*)

Recognition (*anagnorisis*) is moving from a state of ignorance to a state of knowledge and it is inextricably linked with reversal. The example Aristotle uses is when Oedipus realizes who his father is and that the woman he has married is his mother. This sudden realization is important because the audience's pity and fear are incited most effectively through recognition of his mistake, and his own shock at seeing how differently things are to what he thought. In *The Empire Strikes Back*, it is the moment Luke realizes that Darth Vader is telling the truth and that he *is* his father which causes him to pause (and allows Vader to cut off his hand). In *Seven*, recognition is when both David Mills and William Somerset recognize at different moments in the film which sin each murder represents. This builds up as the plot plays out, reaching one final twist at the end. With the symbolism of the final two murders revealed in the final few moments of the film, the tragedy climaxes, as the two detectives realize too late that they represent the final two sins of envy and wrath.

There are various kinds of recognition, according to Aristotle, which playwrights and filmmakers can use to develop the tragedy and the drama in their work:

> **Recognition by marks or objects**: this is where recognition happens through birthmarks or scars, but Aristotle considers this to be the least artistic, showing a lack of imagination in the writer.
>
> **Recognition by memory**, where something triggers a recognition.
>
> **Recognition by deduction** is one of the most artistic because it involves thinking hard.

The best tragedy makes the audience think hard about the plot and deduce what is happening by themselves. We can see this used most obviously in thrillers and detective stories and it works best when combined with reversal. In the film *The Usual Suspects* (1995), the audience must work out a complicated and misleading plot. Right at the moment when we think that we have worked out who the villain is, there is a reversal which takes us totally by surprise. Recognition by deduction is the best form of recognition when it fits seamlessly and logically into the plot. The revelation at the end of *The Usual Suspects* might have audiences baffled for a moment, but the film flashes back to the relevant scenes so that the audience is guided through the steps to draw the correct inference about who the villain is. In this way, the denouement becomes completely logical.

The Importance of Plot

Aristotle identifies six elements of tragedy: plot, character, language, thought, spectacle and song. Unsurprisingly, given his passion for logic and form, Aristotle considers plot the most important. It is through its plot, he suggests, that tragedy will be complete and perform its function. One of the best-known adages by screenwriters and teachers of creative writing is that you should be able to reduce the plot into a paragraph of a few sentences (Aristotle does this with the *Odyssey*). The idea is that the core plot should be clear and precise, and this enables the author to build in the complexity and the sub plots.

The plot, in its simplest form, will focus on a central character who will be someone, a man or woman, of good fortune and position who will fall into misfortune through some mistake. Every play should consist of a complication (*desis*) which leads to the moment of reversal (*peripeteia*) and then the denouement (lusis). Aristotle has, essentially, outlined the basic story arc that is still followed by nearly every screenplay, play or novel. In Chapters 7 and 8 of the *Poetics*, Aristotle elaborates on this idea, suggesting that the plot must be substantial and have orderly arrangement of parts in order to be understood by the observer.

The length of a play or performance should be defined by the nature of events and the natural boundaries of the plot rather than trying to fit into an imposed timeframe.

It's difficult to think of a film or play that does not follow this pattern. Every film in the Marvel universe from *Ironman* (2008) to *Avengers: Endgame* (2019) can be reduced to the core idea: evil villain threatens earth, flawed hero fights to save earth, flawed hero ultimately wins. Naturally the basic plot is extended with sub plot (romance, sidekicks, development of weapons etc.) and made more complex, but the essential story remains the same. This idea of plot leads to the next element that Aristotle argues for.

Unity of Action

Unity refers to the idea of unity of action, where the play, screenplay or novel tells one unified story with a beginning, middle and end. All the sequence of events should fit together logically and be believable. The events in the story should follow on from one another and the author should try not to rely on chance or some sort of divine intervention to tie events together.

This is not to say that the plot should be simple – it should be complex, but it needs to be credible. The audience needs to believe that the events depicted could happen together and in that sequence. Aristotle made clear that there is nothing more irritating in a plot than when, suddenly out of the blue, something happens which is so unlikely as to be unbelievable, a character acts completely out of character, or a villain has a sudden change of heart in order for the plot to work. This creates a disjointed series of events and results in an unsatisfying story.

Epic Poetry

Aristotle spends most of the *Poetics* on tragedy, but in the last few chapters he talks about the other great literary tradition of the Greeks: epic poetry. This art form uses imitation in verse where events are described rather than shown. Like tragedy it has a single sequence of events with a beginning, middle and end, giving it an organic unity. For Aristotle, Homer surpasses all other writers. In the *Iliad*, Homer does not try to cover all the events of the Trojan War but concentrates on the events that lead Achilles to withdraw from the fighting and then return. Like tragedy, the epic should be based on character and suffering and include recognition and reversal; it can be in the form of a simple plot (the *Iliad*) or a more complex one (the *Odyssey*).

The difference between epic and tragedy is in its length and its use of verse. Epics, such as the *Iliad* and *Odyssey* are around 15,000 lines whereas a play might be between 5,000 and 6,000. This gives epic an advantage: its length allows it to present events that happen simultaneously and to create a sense of grandeur. Despite this advantage, however, Aristotle considers tragedy to be superior to epic. A drama, he argues, contains all the elements of epic with the addition of music and the stage show itself. The vividness of the play produces an intense artistic pleasure.

Rhetoric

Dr Martin Luther King's famous speech, 'I have a Dream', in 1963, is one of the most well-known and recognizable examples of public speaking in the Western world. Dr King's words not only inspired the thousands at the Lincoln Memorial in Washington, D.C., USA, but have continued to inspire passion and action against inequality in the years since. The speech is an excellent example of what Aristotle called rhetoric:

> '*I am happy to join with you today in what will go down in history as the greatest demonstration for freedom in the history of our nation. Five score years ago, a great American, in whose symbolic shadow we stand today, signed the Emancipation Proclamation. This momentous decree came as a great beacon light of hope to millions of Negro slaves who had been seared in the flames of withering injustice. It came as a joyous daybreak to end the long night of their captivity.*' (King, 1963)

Rhetoric is the art of effective or persuasive speaking or writing and Aristotle has been credited with developing the basic system of rhetoric that has come down to us today. Rhetoric is necessary because people need to be able to persuade each other through reason and fine argument in a variety of situations: political, social, religious and legal.

Rhetoric, like poetry, was another area of disagreement between Plato and Aristotle. Plato loathed rhetoric (which is ironic as many of his works display a fine use of rhetoric). In the *Gorgias* Plato describes it as a form of flattery. He argued that rhetoric has potential for both harm and for good and he saw it as a knack rather than a true art – a skill that one has come by naturally rather than through study of what the truth really is. He sought to distinguish sophists from philosophers, arguing that a sophist was a person who made his living through deception, whereas a philosopher was a lover of wisdom who sought the truth. One of the main reasons that the sophists were looked down upon is because they charged money for their teaching and were employed by the wealthy to teach their sons. The word 'sophist' refers to a class of itinerant intellectuals who taught courses in various subjects, speculated about the nature of language and culture, and employed rhetoric to persuade or convince others.

Aristotle took a different view. He argued that rhetoric was essential to philosophy and to other fields of study as well. In many situations we need the skill of persuasion, for example a doctor needs to persuade a patient to accept her diagnosis, a politician needs to persuade people to vote, an actor to persuade the audience to accept his character, even in day-to-day situations we seek to persuade or to influence others to do, say or think a multitude of things.

Aristotle asks: What is a good speech? What do popular audiences find persuasive? How does one compose a persuasive speech? Aristotle considers these questions in the context of the Greek city-state, in which large audiences of ordinary citizens listened to speeches for and against before casting their votes. Persuasion by means of the spoken word was the vehicle for conducting politics and administering the law (Kennedy, 1991).

Aristotle acknowledged that the goal of rhetoric is persuasion, not truth, and therefore techniques of rhetoric could be bent to immoral or dishonest ends. Nonetheless, he insists that it is in the public interest to provide a comprehensive and systematic survey of the field.

Creating a Good Argument

The dialectic, like rhetoric, is a form of philosophical argument through questioning. The dialectic expects us to reach a conclusion based solely on the success of the argument. Rhetoric uses more emotion and, rather than seeking to find the truth, it seeks to get people to agree with you which may result in a proximation of the truth rather than the truth itself. The dialectic is a more scientific argument while rhetoric appeals to the emotions. However, as with his other works, Aristotle treated rhetoric like a science and in his treatise, *Rhetoric*, he categorizes, divides and defines the subject in various ways.

In order to create a good argument Aristotle contends that we need to consider three things: the character of the speaker, the condition of the listener and the strength of the argument. In terms of character, clearly an intelligent, virtuous speaker will inspire confidence and win over the listeners. A good speaker will consider the condition of his listeners and craft an argument that soothes people's fears and identifies what is at stake for the listeners. We also have to acknowledge that people have a short attention span, Aristotle argues, and therefore we need to use humour or wit to keep the audience's attention.

Finally, a good persuasive argument must still make use of the same rules that make a good philosophical or scientific argument. We need to identify premises that are true, demonstrable and help to construct the argument, so that they naturally support a conclusion. Aristotle reminds us that just because a message suggests that a text will be interpreted in a certain way, it does not always mean that it will be. A message can be interpreted in more than one way, therefore, if the speaker wants an audience to interpret a message in a particular way, it is important to understand the audience.

Means of Persuasion

Aristotle also distinguishes between three means of persuasion: *ethos, logos* and *pathos*. Ethos refers to the underlying sentiment that informs the beliefs of a group. Therefore, in terms of Aristotle's means of persuasion, ethos is how you convince an audience of your credibility; you need to understand morality and be able to convince an audience that, not only do you know what you are talking about, but that they themselves are good, trustworthy people worth listening to (ethos). We might call this ability charisma.

Logos is the use of logic and reason. In an ideal situation the argument would be so overwhelmingly logical that it would be able to persuade on its own. But the argument still can't be truly persuasive without the credibility of the speaker and the right emotional attitude of the audience. In order to achieve logos, the speaker needs to prove something to the audience so that it can be presented as factual and therefore persuasive. This method can employ rhetorical devices such as analogies, examples, and citations of research or statistics. But it's not just facts and figures. It's also the structure and content of the speech itself. The point is to use factual knowledge to convince the audience but, unfortunately, speakers can also manipulate people with false information that the audience thinks is true. This is particularly true in our society today where 'fake news' has become a common tool of persuasion.

Finally, pathos appeals to emotions. How successfully an argument persuades an audience depends on the emotions of the audience: emotions have an important effect on our decisions and therefore it is important for the speaker to control these emotions. This is where Aristotle argues that the sophists failed to create perfection in their rhetoric. He believed that they created rhetoric solely through pathos whereas they needed to add logos. Aristotle vastly improved on the stylized devices used by the sophists by systemizing and categorizing the art of rhetoric.

Donald Trump's inaugural speech in January 2017 demonstrates much of what Aristotle is talking about. He clearly uses pathos in appealing to the emotions of his supporters and he couches his argument in what seems like logic, particularly in the following section where he seems to have identified what was wrong at the heart of government and then draws on the emotions of his listeners to give them what he promises – power.

> 'For too long, a small group in our nation's Capital has reaped the rewards of government while the people have borne the cost. Washington flourished – but the people did not share in its wealth. Politicians prospered – but the jobs left, and the factories closed. The establishment protected itself, but not the citizens of our country. Their victories have not been your victories; their triumphs have not been your triumphs; and while they celebrated in our nation's capital, there was little to celebrate for struggling families all across our land.
>
> That all changes – starting right here, and right now, because this moment is your moment: it belongs to you. It belongs to everyone gathered here today and everyone watching all across America. This is your day. This is your celebration. And this, the United States of America, is your country.
>
> What truly matters is not which party controls our government, but whether our government is controlled

by the people. January 20, 2017, will be remembered as
the day the people became the rulers of this nation again.'

Trump's speech demonstrates the importance of persuasion that Aristotle emphasizes. Persuasiveness must come from the speaker themselves; it's the way they convince the audience that is the key to success, and we see that in Trump's body language and his use of the finger to punctuate his points. Aristotle views persuasion flexibly, examining how speakers should devise arguments, evoke emotions, and demonstrate their own credibility. Aristotle's treatise has had a profound influence on later attempts to understand what makes speech persuasive and we can see the results in modern advertising, in politics, and in any area of life where persuasion is needed. Techniques such as list making, or repetition are also examples of persuasion. Martin Luther King was the master of repetition. In his Washington speech of 28 August 1963, he used the phrases 'I have a dream' and 'Let freedom ring' seven times and eight times respectively.

The use of three-part lists is also a common technique, as we can see in Trump's inaugural address above when he says 'This is your day. This is your celebration. And this, the United States of America, is your country'. Another example is Abraham Lincoln's Gettysburg Address – the speech he made during the American Civil War – where he says, 'government of the people, by the people, and for the people' (Lincoln, 1863). Tony Blair, the former British Prime Minister, was particularly fond of using this technique as well as also using an attention-seeking phrase, such as 'I say this to you' – which was one of his favourites.

There are, according to Aristotle, six 'rules' for creating a successful argument. The first is where the argument is situated. Once we understand where the speech is situated then we need to understand the context. How do we create a persuasive argument? Aristotle lays it out as follows. The first step is to figure out what you are going to say in order to support a message: What lines of argument and what evidence will you use? Then you need to think about the arrangement: What order are the points going to be in to make the argument more logical? Style comes next in the use of language to frame your point in a way that the audience will understand, but also, you need to deliver it in a way that will keep the audience engaged. Again, Trump's use of body language is an excellent example of this. The fifth rule is memory – learning mnemonic devices so that one could deliver a speech without notes. Former British Prime Minister David Cameron's speech to the conservative party conference in 2005 is noteworthy because he spoke without notes which probably helped him in becoming a front runner in the conservative leadership contest. The final rule is the delivery: considering how you are going to use your voice and body to convey your message to the audience. Modern speechmakers spend a great deal of time with their advisers working out their delivery, the soundbite, and the way to pitch their ideas to an audience.

A speech delivered in an assembly or a trial is, Aristotle argues, of a particular kind. The speaker's purpose is either to defend someone or to prosecute someone; to persuade an audience of either guilt or innocence; or to persuade the audience of the rightness of a particular action. Socrates' speech at his trial is a good example, or Atticus Finch's closing speech at the trial of Tom

Robinson in Harper Lee's novel *To Kill a Mockingbird* (1960). In the film version of the book, we can see here how Finch fulfils all the criteria that Aristotle set out for the best rhetoric: it has a clear logic, it uses repetition, three-part lists and pauses, to name a few:

> '*Thomas Jefferson once said that all men are created equal, a phrase that the Yankees and the distaff side [...] are fond of hurling at us. There is a tendency in this year of grace, 1935, for certain people to use that phrase out of context, to satisfy all conditions [...] We know that all men are not created equal in the sense that some people would have us believe. Some people are smarter than others, some people have more opportunity because they are born with it, some men have more money than others, and some people are more gifted than others. But there is one way in this country in which all men are created equal. An institution that makes a pauper the equal of a Rockefeller, the ignorant man the equal of any college president, and the stupid man the equal of Einstein. That institution is the court [...] But a court is only as sound as its jury, and the jury is only as sound as the men who make it up. I am confident that you gentlemen will review without passion the evidence you have heard, come to a decision, and restore the defendant to his family. In the name of God, do your duty. In the name of God, believe Tom Robinson.*' (*To Kill a Mockingbird*, 1962)

The speech also has the key ingredients: using pathos, Finch makes an emotional connection with the audience; he has ethos, the credibility of being a lawyer and a respected member of the community; and above all, the speech demonstrates logos: logical analysis and clear argument, particularly when he acknowledges that men are not created equal – in a court room equality is everything. I think Aristotle would have approved.

Conclusion

ristotle died more than 2,300 years ago and yet he remains one of the most influential and important thinkers and for this reason alone we should continue to read him and investigate his ideas. Aristotle's influence has been felt in both Western and Eastern traditions and it is to Muslim scholars that we must give thanks for their preservation of the works of Aristotle that have survived, in particular to Ya'qub ibn Ishaq al-Sabah al-Kindi (c. 800–870) a major philosopher in his own right who led a group of early translators responsible for preserving much of Aristotle's work. Aristotle is considered the father of Western logic and his works cover every field from biology and physics to astronomy, psychology and logic. As far as we know from the writings that survive, he was the first to ground his ideas in experimentation and physical investigation rather than abstract thought. He developed the first system of scientific classification which helped later biologists to categorize plant and animal species. But should we only read Aristotle because of his status as an ancient philosopher or has he got something to say about modern life?

Edith Hall (2019) argues that Aristotle is 'quite simply the most important intellectual who ever lived'. He thought everyone from the greatest intellectual to a peasant farmer was capable of reason and deliberation and he wrote for everyone, not just academics and students (however it has to be acknowledged that women and slaves were not his intended audience). He felt that he had something important to say about the human condition which could help people lead a better life then and now. The *Nicomachean Ethics*, as we have seen, shows how good Aristotle was at understanding human happiness and giving us a guide to good living. The *Ethics* are like an ancient self-help manual which can meet the modern need for guidance and moral understanding without the need to believe in a 'God'. The responsibility for leading a good life (eudaimonia) is our own. If we think back to his view that eudaimonia is something that is brought about by habit and practice, we can see what an attractive idea it is for modern audiences who want a secular approach to what it is to be 'good'. Aristotle's emphasis on fulfilling your individual potential as well as engaging with family, friends and other citizens to create a mutually beneficial society offers us an attainable way for our communities to progress.

His views on education, that it should be public and developed to prepare citizens to take part in a society and the political system, chime with our own views. He argued that education would enable young people to become free citizens, free from the negative influence of those who seek to persuade us of their views. Aristotle wants us to think for ourselves; to be able to engage with the political system to ensure that it promotes the common good. He argued that education should provide us with the opportunities to appreciate and understand all the things that enrich life. Whether that is having an appreciation of music or knowing how to read and write in order to communicate and gain an understanding of literature, film or art. He also advocated a similar understanding of the sciences that allows us to see how physics, biology, sociology, mathematics, psychology etc. work to create the complexities of our natural and social world.

We could even argue that Aristotle is the father of capitalism. In the *Politics*, he asserted that the purpose of society is to enable each member 'to attain a higher and better life by the mutual exchange of their different services'. Aristotle is promoting the entrepreneurial idea that has kick-started the internet, tech companies and a thousand start-ups; that has led to innovation in science, and technology and society, although he might not have seen Instagram and the rise of the 'influencer' as something positive. His vision of an education that aims at giving us a better understanding of the things that create freedom and richness in our lives could create a very different (and more positive) society from the one we have now.

If your interest in Aristotle's ideas have been piqued, then where to go next? You might want to read Aristotle for yourself and, although some complain that his work is dense and can be difficult to read, his ideas are worth the effort and there are some excellent translations available. As we have covered only a few of his theories here, you might want to investigate his ideas on politics, or logic, or look more deeply at his works on biology and the sciences. His influence on later thinkers has been huge and it would also be worth investigating his influence in the area of cosmology, with the works of St Thomas Aquinas in particular or arguments about mind and body: the modern materialist theories of Daniel Dennett or David Chalmers (whose naturalistic dualist philosophy is closer to Aristotle's than Dennett's) would complement Aristotle's ideas. Or see how modern virtue ethicists such as Philippa Foot or Alasdair McIntyre have taken ideas of virtue and reimagined them for the twentieth and twenty-first century.

Whichever approach you choose, you won't be disappointed. In opposition to the rule-based theories of Kant or the utilitarian position of Bentham and Mill, Aristotle's writing touches on every aspect of the human condition and still has much to say on the subject.

Appendix: Who the hell are they?

The following is a list of names referred to in this book:

Alexander the Great: son of Philip II and ascendent to the throne in 336 BCE

Amyntas III: king of Macedonia

Anaxagoras of Clazomenae: pre-Socratic philosopher

Anaximander of Miletus: pre-Socratic philosopher, student of Thales

Anaximenes of Miletus: pre-Socratic philosopher, friend or student of Anaximander

Arimneste: Aristotle's older sister

Callisthenes: Aristotle's great nephew, son of Hero

Democritus: pre-Socratic philosopher and atomist, student of Leucippus

Eudoxus of Cnidus: Aristotle's teacher at the Academy, student of Plato

Heraclitus of Ephesus: pre-Socratic philosopher

Hermias: ruler of Atarneus

Hero: Arimneste's daughter and the mother of Callisthenes

Herpyllis: Aristotle's female companion

Leucippus: pre-Socratic philosopher and atomist

Nicanor: Arimneste's son

Nichomachus the elder: Aristotle's father, a court physician

Nichomachus the younger: Aristotle's son, by Herpyllis

Parmenides: pre-Socratic philosopher, founder of the Eleatic School

Phaestis: Aristotle's mother

Philip II: Amyntas III's son, who succeeded his father in 359 BCE

Plato: Athenian philosopher and Aristotle's teacher and mentor

Proxenus of Atarneus: Aristotle's guardian and Arimneste's husband

Pythagoras: pre-Socratic philosopher

Pythias the elder: Aristotle's wife, niece of Hermias

Pythias the younger: Aristotle's daughter, by Pythias

Socrates: Athenian philosopher and teacher to Plato and Xenophon

Speusippus: Plato's nephew, successor to Plato's Academy

Thales of Miletus: pre-Socratic philosopher, mathematician and astronomer

Theophrastus: Plato's student, then Aristotle's student, successor to the Lyceum

Xenophanes: pre-Socratic philosopher, teacher of Zeno, colleague of Parmenides

Xenophon: student of Socrates

Zeno: pre-Socratic philosopher, a member of the Eleatic School, founded by Parmenides

Bibliography

Works by Aristotle

Aristotle, *Politics*, translated by Ernest Barker, Oxford World Classics, 2009.

Aristotle, *Ethics*, translated by W.D. Ross, Oxford World Classics, 2009.

Aristotle, *Poetics*, translated by Anthony Kenny, Oxford World Classics, 2013.

Aristotle, *The Art of Rhetoric*, translated by Robin Waterfield, Oxford World Classics, 2018.

Aristotle, *On the Soul and Other Psychological Works*, translated by Fred D. Miller, Oxford World Classics, 2018.

Other works cited

Ackrill, J.L. (1981) *Aristotle the Philosopher*, Oxford: Oxford University Press.

Ackrill, J.L. (1988) *A New Aristotle Reader*, Princeton University Press.

Annas, J. (1988) *Metaphysics Books M and N*, Translated with a commentary, Oxford: Oxford University Press.

Annas, J (2006) 'Virtue Ethics' in Copp, D (ed.) *The Oxford Handbook of Ethical Theory*, Oxford: Oxford University Press.

Barnes, Jonathan (1986) *Aristotle (Past Masters)*, Oxford University Press.

Blunden, Andy (2005) *Philosophical Foundations*, ebook accessed 18 December 2019. Available at: https://www.ethicalpolitics.org/ablunden/works/aristotle.htm

Curd, Patricia (2019) 'Pre-Socratic Philosophy', in Zalta, Edward (ed.) *The Stanford Encyclopedia of Philosophy,* Available at: www.plato.stanford.edu

Daiches, David (1981) *Critical Approaches to Literature,* Longman.

Diogenes Laertius (1950) *Lives of Eminent Philosophers,* translated by R. D. Hicks, Volume II, London: Loeb.

Durant, William (1926) *The Story of Philosophy,* Simon and Schuster.

Forshaw, Amanda (2008) *Philosophy A Level Course Materials,* The National Extension College.

Freeman, Kathleen (1946) *The Pre-Socratic Philosophers,* Oxford: Blackwell.

Hall, Edith (2018) 'Why read Aristotle today?' *Aeon,* 1 June.

Hall, Edith (2019) *Aristotle's Way: How Ancient Wisdom Can Change Your Life,* Penguin.

Halliwell, Stephen (1998) *Aristotle's Poetics,* Chicago: University of Chicago Press.

Hursthouse, Rosalind (2001) *On Virtue Ethics,* Oxford University Press.

In Our Time: 'Socrates' (2007) BBC Radio 4, 27 September.

In Our Time: 'Aristotle Politics' (2008) BBC Radio 4, 6 November.

In Our Time: 'Aristotle and Biology' (2019) BBC Radio 4, 17 February.

Irwin, Terence H. (1991) 'Aristotle's philosophy of mind', in Everson, Stephen (ed.) *Psychology. Vol. 2 of Companions to ancient thought,* pp.56–83. Cambridge University Press.

Johnson, Monte Ransome (2006) *Aristotle on Teleology,* Oxford Scholarship Online.

Kennedy, G. E. (1991) *Aristotle, On Rhetoric, a Theory of Civic Discourse,* Oxford University Press.

King, Martin Luther Jr. (1963) Extract from 'I Have a Dream,' delivered 28 August 1963, at the Lincoln Memorial, Washington D.C. Available at: https://www.americanrhetoric.com/speeches/mlkihaveadream.htm Accessed 20 March, 2020.

Kirwan, C. (1993) *Metaphysics: Books gamma, delta, and epsilon,* Second Edition, Translated with notes, Oxford: Oxford University Press.

Lawson-Tancred, Hugh (2017) *The Art of Rhetoric, Aristotle,* Penguin.

Lincoln, Abraham (1863) 'Gettysburg Address', available at: https://en.wikipedia.org/wiki/Gettysburg_Address Accessed: 20 May, 2020.

Lowe, N. J. (2000) *The Classical Plot and the Invention of Western Narrative,* Cambridge University Press.

MacIntyre, Alasdair, (1999) *Dependent Rational Animals: Why Human Beings Need the Virtues,* London: Duckworth.

Madigan, A. (2000) *Aristotle: Metaphysics Books B and K 1–2,* translated with a commentary, Oxford: Oxford University Press.

Magee, Bryan talks to Martha Nussbaum about Aristotle (1987) BBC Education and Training. Available at: http://www.openculture.com/2012/05/bryan_magees_in-depth_uncut_tv_conversations_with_famous_philosophers_1978-87.html Accessed 20 March, 2020.

Makin, S. (2006) *Metaphysics Theta,* translated with an introduction and commentary, Oxford: Oxford University Press.

McKirahan, Richard D. (2010) *Philosophy Before Socrates: An Introduction with Texts and Commentaries.* Indianapolis: Hackett Publishing.

McLeish, Kenneth (1999) *Aristotle,* Routledge.

Nussbaum, Martha C., and Amélie Oksenberg Rorty, eds. (1995) *Essays on Aristotle's De anima.* Oxford: Clarendon.

Rackham, H. (1959) *Aristotle,* Harvard University Press.

Reeve, C.D.C. (2019) 'The well-educated person', *Aeon,* 23 September.

Stewart, N. (2008) *Ethics: An Introduction to Moral Philosophy,* Polity Press.

Trump, Donald (2017) 'The full text of Donald Trump's inaugural speech', *The Guardian*, Friday 20 January 2017. Available at: https://www.theguardian.com/world/2017/jan/20/donald-trump-inauguration-speech-full-text Accessed 20 March 2020.

To Kill a Mockingbird (1962) Directed by Robert Mulligan [Film]. United States, Brentwood Productions and Pakula-Mulligan. Excerpt from film taken from *American Rhetoric Movie Speeches*, available at: https://www.americanrhetoric.com/MovieSpeeches/moviespeechtokillamockingbird.html Accessed 20 March 2020.

Waldemar Heckel and J.C. Yardley (2003) *Historical Sources in Translation: Alexander the Great,* Wiley and Sons.

Biography

Amanda Forshaw is head of Philosophy and Religious Studies at a north London Sixth Form College as well as a senior examiner on the Philosophy A level. She has spent the last 10 years, alongside teaching, writing revision guides and course material for Hodder Education. She is passionate about philosophy, political philosophy and social contract theory. Amanda lives in Cumbria, England.

Acknowledgements

For Lucas.

Picture Credits:

Who the hell is

This exciting new series of books sets out to explore the life and theories of the world's leading intellectuals in a clear and understandable way. The series currently includes the following subject areas:

Art History | Psychology | Philosophy | Sociology | Politics

Available now:

For more information about forthcoming titles in the Who the hell is...? series, go to: **www.whothehellis.co.uk**.

If any of our readers would like to put in a request for a particular intellectual to be included in our series, then please contact us at **info@whothehellis.co.uk**.

Made in United States
North Haven, CT
25 September 2022

24536232R00071